# Survive to Thrive

# LEGAL NOTICES

# Survive to Thrive

*Five Steps To Growing Your Dream Business*

## Alan S Adams

# "Claim Your <u>FREE</u> Business Builder Tools For Use In Your Business and Increase Your Turnover by 50% to 100% Without Spending More Money On Advertising!"

*(£297 Total Value)*

### *Details revealed below...*

**Alan S Adams,** author and leading business consultant, is offering an incredible opportunity for you to improve the way you run your business, without spending more money on advertising, for <u>FREE</u>! Alan has used these systems to help businesses grow for years, and he is so confident that they work, he always offers a **"500% Return On Investment or Your Money Back Guarantee"**. So claim your free tools today and discover:

- How to **quickly increase your sales by 50% to 100%** without spending more money on advertising

- How to **guarantee that your business grows** with small changes achieving huge returns

- The **"Five Simple Steps"** to get you a plan, really get you focused, and get you building the lifestyle you deserve

- **Secret insider tips and techniques** to get more new customers, and get your past customers to come back into your business and buy from you again and again

- How to get **Free Business Building** tools that have helped countless other businesses grow, and that Alan uses with his private clients.

*Claim Your FREE Tools by Visiting:*

## www.alansadams.com/free

# TABLE OF CONTENTS

## PART ONE:

# INTRODUCTION

I t's amazing to see the variety of people in business today. Advances in technology, new franchise systems, innovative business opportunities, or simply just the fact that someone is really good at what they do and believe that they can do it better than their employer, have all meant that we've seen an explosion in the number of people taking the plunge and launching their own business.

But this has also lead to an incredibly high mortality rate, and a veritable graveyard of failed businesses from the last few years alone. The main reason? No one was taught at school or college how to actually run a business, how to employ people, how important cash flow is, how to implement a practical marketing plan, how to generate sales in the real world, or how to set out and communicate your vision… Let alone any one of about fifty other essential tasks that any business owner has to get absolutely right in order to be ultimately successful.

And if you're thinking 'hey, I'll go and get an MBA from a business school and learn all that I need', well Tony Hsieh, CEO of Zappos (which sold to Amazon at a value of $1.2 billion in 2009) made an interesting comparison between an entrepreneur and someone who'd been through business school when he explained that an entrepreneur will, if they have to make something to eat, go to the kitchen to get whatever ingredients there are and make something, while your business school MBA will go find a recipe then go out shopping for the correct ingredients. What a great way to define what makes an entrepreneur different!

An entrepreneur will always be looking at other ways to grow their business. A true entrepreneur may move from owning one shop, to another, and another, before focusing on becoming a supplier to other shops, and onwards. A business owner, however, would be content with owning and running his business himself, and with being master of his own destiny. Both are great, and this book has been designed to help you, whichever type you are, in fact I'll refer to you both as we move through the book.

When first getting into business a lot of people make a small number of common mistakes, but the problems really arise when they *continue* making them because – let's face it – we don't know what we don't know. And that's where this book is going to help you. Whether you're a brand new start-up or you've been in business for years, the techniques you'll learn here will help catapult your business to success.

Because – don't forget – being good at what you do is no guarantee of business success. I've spoken to countless people who believe that just being good will lead to them being discovered, bought out, or chosen in some way, and their business worries being over. This couldn't be further from the truth. While there'll always be the odd person where this might happen – hey, even the lottery gets won – on the whole this is a disastrous strategy, and if it feels familiar then you need to change and fast.

The variety of different roles or 'hats' that you need to wear within any business can be just overwhelming, and many business owners and entrepreneurs freeze before they even start. When I'm giving talks I often share the tale of the university lecturer who, in front of his students produces a large glass jar that he fills with golf balls. He then asks his students "is the jar full?" The students all agree that the jar is full but the lecturer then pulls some marbles out from under the desk and pours them into the jar...

The marbles fill the gaps between the golf balls, and again, the lecturer asks "is the jar full". Once more the students agree that yes the jar is definitely now full, but the lecturer pulls out a bag of sand and proceeds to pour that into the jar too. He again asks the students "is the jar full" and the students – who by this point are less inclined to say it is, sit quietly. The lecturer then pulls out a beaker of water and tips the water in the jar and again asks if the jar is full...

He points out that life is very like the jar – the important things are the golf balls and the marbles, with the sand and the water representing the other activities that we get involved with. If you're not careful, you can fill your jar with sand and water and leave no room for the important stuff. Business is the same. Too often we get wrapped up in the actual doing – serving the customer, making the widget, processing the sale – and not working on the important things which will actually grow our business into something that supports us moving forwards.

When I'm working with groups, given the chance I always ask the question "what makes a person successful?" Regardless of who I'm working with, there's always a long list: confidence, happiness, focus, a positive attitude, great communication skills, a good work ethic, luck, charisma, consistency... The list goes on, but the results are always the same. When you look at the attributes of a successful person and break them down into zones, 10%

will always focus on features which relate to the person's mind and intellect, 10% will be skills-based, and the great news is that a whopping 80% will be attitude-based.

And that's great news because *you* decide your attitude, and it's your attitude that will pretty much determine your skill level, intelligence and ultimately how successful you are. The right attitude will establish your discipline and your ability to follow through on what this book will teach you. Decide now to take action and commit to giving yourself, your family, and the people important to you, the life you all deserve.

# CHAPTER 1

## The Essential Ingredients

I ride an old 1978 Triumph Bonneville and I've spent thousands of pounds and hundreds of hours on it, making it go quicker, improving the handling and – importantly with an old bike – making it brake better. I've even had it out on a few track days chasing much more modern bikes. Riding a bike is a skill and it's something that I'm OK at. I just love going out for a ride and getting in the zone where you're completely engaged in the present moment and you simply don't think about anything else. Buddhists would refer to it as mindfulness and living exactly in the present, I just think of the huge smile I always have on my face.

But it makes me really marvel at just how incredible professional bike racers are – they almost seem to defy the laws of gravity, and their focus is something every business owner and entrepreneur can learn from. I've been to the Isle of Man TT races a few times (if you've never heard of the TT races do look them up, it's road racing at the extreme). Motorbikes touch nearly 200mph and race around a 37.9 mile track made up of the island's own roads, which in all honesty are at best just B roads, complete with all of the street furniture, telegraph poles, walls and even houses you'd expect. If you've never seen any footage of these races you can see some bike camera shots on YouTube, and it just shows the speeds which are phenomenal. Anyway, how these racers learn this incredibly long and complicated track, and how they take in such a huge amount of information at the speed they're going is truly amazing. Of course, at these speeds, and on these roads, when something goes wrong it tends to go very badly wrong for the rider.

I recall an interview with a racer called Guy Martin who was entered into the senior race at the TT a couple of years ago. Guy, an experienced racer, had complained that the front tyre kept pattering in corners at high speed (pattering means the tyre was ever so slightly bouncing and leaving the tarmac for a fraction of a second) which caused the bike to run wide – not good on a narrow road with brick walls and telegraph poles, at these incredible speeds. Just so that you can understand how the races work, basically, if you live in the Isle of Man during these events you tend to leave the island as it's invaded by 40,000 bike fanatics who get to watch their race heroes while they stand on the roadside, a mere 10 feet away from them in places. It's a great atmosphere with everyone wanting these heroes to come in safely, and glued to their radios listening to the commentary…

Anyway, Guy set off on the race and was doing well until he hit his third lap where he came into Ballagarey Corner at 150mph and the front end of the bike started to wash out. A split second later the commentator was reporting a huge fire ball at Ballagarey and everybody's heart sank. Everyone on the island knew that this was the fastest corner of the track, and that Guy, if not killed instantly was almost definitely critically injured. Even his pit crew, believing him dead, started packing his belongings in the garage away. However, on the run into the corner, Guy had what every successful person has, complete focus... In the split second that the bike started to run wide, Guy was focusing on where he wanted to go and, knowing he was heading for a wall, actually started to leap from the bike in an effort to stay on line.

Guy suffered broken ribs, bruised lungs, twisted ankles and fractured vertebrae, which is the equivalent of a scratch considering the speed at which the crash took place! The key factor that kept Guy alive? His absolute, unwavering focus.

OK, so focus keeps us alive and it keeps us on track, but it also builds successful businesses, glittering careers, great lifestyles, Olympic-medal-winning athletes, and history-making teams. You're sat there now and you've got focus, or you're working towards it, but what exactly should you be focused on? Well, as a business owner or entrepreneur have you ever had a pile of jobs to do and simply not been sure where to start? Let's face it, many people could work seven days a week, 20 hours a day, but still seem to generate more work. They start feeling completely overwhelmed and don't feel like they're getting anywhere despite the hours and effort they've put into their business.

And why? Simply because they lack the key ingredient in business... A plan.

Without a plan how can you possibly know what to focus on? Without a plan how can you avoid being a busy fool? Someone who's working really hard with their head down, simply ploughing through stuff, and never looking up to see where they're going. All of which reminds me of a friend of mine called Johnny. Johnny comes from a farming background and he was telling me how when he was a youngster his brother taught him to plough a field. He got him in the tractor and told him to concentrate on the front wheel and keep that in the furrow of what had already been done, which was a dead straight line. Johnny ran the full length of the field and when he got to the end, his brother told him to look behind him at what he'd ploughed.

Johnny turned and saw something that was about as far from a straight line as you could possibly get. So, Johnny's brother took over, straightened up the furrow and put Johnny back in the driver seat. This time he said "watch the wheel and keep it in the furrow but also pick a spot on the horizon directly in front and keep an eye on that". Again, Johnny ran the full length of the field, looking to the horizon and keeping an eye on the wheel in the furrow. This time, when he got to the end and turned around to look, he'd ploughed a perfectly straight line.

And that's how everything works, no matter what it is you're trying to achieve, you have to look to where you're going, as well as have an eye on what's going on now. I see too many business owners who not only don't have a plan for the now, but aren't really clear about where they're going either. And that's a bit like deciding to go on holiday, turning up to any old airport, pointing at an aeroplane and saying "that one will do", and all without even having your passport or a suitcase. Actually, the average person probably spends more time planning their holidays than they do planning their life, which is clearly a completely bonkers way of doing things!

Johnny went on to enjoy a high-powered career in the corporate world before starting his own consultancy, GOOD2GREAT, with his business partner Gary. They've shared a few tools with me for reference in this book so I wanted to take the opportunity to pass on my thanks.

Anyway, if you're sitting there thinking "well I know what I want and where I want to go" well done, that's fantastic, and it's a great start. But have you written it down? Is it on a single piece of paper with a rough plan showing what's going to be happening in each area of your business for the next five years, and do you have a concise two page action plan breaking down what you need to do, with each task prioritised in order of when it needs doing? If you can answer yes, then well done you! That's absolutely fantastic and if you read the rest of the book I'm positive you'll gain a few additional nuggets.

And do share your feedback or anything that you think I could improve on – it would be gratefully received.

For the other 96% of us, that's what this book is here to help you do. The whole point is to help you work out exactly what you want to achieve, not simply in your business but across all areas of your life. We can then look at how your business is going to supply you with that lifestyle, and we'll devise a strategy and written plan to get you focused and get you there.

Talking about the plan, you may have heard a military saying 'no plan survives first contact with the enemy', well the same is true in business, although it should be modified to 'no plan survives first contact with the customer and competitors'. In *Made To Stick*, Chip and Dan Heath show how some ideas are easy to remember like a bogus scare story, while people often struggle to recall information that may be really important to them. They actually came up with the six factors that make ideas 'sticky' and one of these factors is simplicity.

They give the example that during the 1980s, the military recognised that on the field of battle their plans used to literally get shot to pieces, so they came up with something that could be a lot more flexible and correct the troops on the ground. It was called 'Commanders Intent' or 'CI'. So, instead of trying to have a detailed, formal plan to direct the troops on the ground, in a blow-by-blow exchange with the enemy, the CI would give the idea in its simplest top-line form which everyone could understand. The CI might, for example, be to clear a hill of the enemy and protect the advancement to the east of their position. This direction is so clear that, even if they were down to their last foot soldier, he would still understand what was required of him.

And the same is true in business. Your plan, or CI, is there to guide you and your staff to a specific end point, but it should allow you the flexibility to decide how that end is achieved. Before we jump into building this killer strategy to drive your business forward, the preceding chapters are going to cover a number of areas that are important for ground work and greater understanding to allow you to have the foundations in place to really push things to the next level.

Now, each of these areas area could easily be a book in its own right, but I know that time is precious to you, so I'm going to cover the top-level information that you need to make the maximum difference to your business, here, in this one book. Leaving you free to follow-up with further reading on all or any sections which are particularly pertinent for you.

I've made sure to include some mind stuff, because getting your head in the right place is one of the most important factors, and I've thrown in some opinions of my own, asked you some questions, and made some suggestions too. Some may be new to you, a lot you may know but – and do be honest with yourself – you aren't doing. What I'd love you to avoid though, is reading any one snippet in isolation and implementing it into your business before you've read the rest of the book. I promise you, the content and the structure has all been carefully devised to fit together like a strategic jigsaw, and you won't be doing yourself any favours if you jump ahead.

Please do make notes and highlight stuff. Perhaps use page markers so that you can easily flip back to find the details you want, but please don't do anything until you've completed the simple five step process at the end to decide exactly what you're going to do. OK? Pinky promise?

---

**Chapter Summary**

- Get Focus

- Work on what's important

- Develop a great attitude

- Develop your own 'Commanders Intent'.

---

# CHAPTER 2

## Why Are You Doing This?

Quite often I'll have people ask me "how do I get more customers?" "How do I develop better products?" Or "how do I make a £million?" I always ask "why do you want that?" Often the first answer is "I want more money", but that's not likely to be the important bit, so I'll ask again "why do you want that?" and they start digging around for a compelling reason as to why they're doing what they're doing.

Ever heard the saying 'nothing worth doing is ever easy'? Bombshell alert – if building a business was easy, everyone would do it. It takes a certain amount of courage to become financially responsible for yourself, and it takes even more courage to be disciplined enough to do the things that others aren't willing to do now, to secure your financial future.

And if you're employing staff, you're also financially responsible for them too. Their mortgages rely on your business. If you haven't already been through tough times, you'll probably be in for some, whether its challenges with cash flow, waiting on decisions from others as to whether you get that dream business deal, or just plain and simply being let down by people.

You're likely to wake up in the middle of the night at some point worrying. You may feel stressed and lacking energy, and you might even be thinking "I'm not sure how much more of this I can take" or even "is it all worth it". Well, you're not alone. Literally every successful business owner has been through this. Richard Branson has walked the streets of London at 3am because he was worried about what was going on within one of his businesses. Ultimately though, we all need to learn that if it's within your control, do something about, and if it isn't, stop worrying about it and focus on something that you can affect.

There are actually two 'why's' you need to know to make building your successful business easier. The first is 'why are you doing this'? What's in it for you? What is your end goal on a personal level? So, basically consider what lifestyle you want, where you want to live, where you want to travel, who you want to help, how many holidays you want to take, how many days a week you want to work...

And this is important on a couple of levels. Firstly, if you don't know what your end goal is, you can end up anywhere, and anywhere might not be a place you like very much. And secondly, your brain is incredibly powerful and so you need it to be on your side. Quite often people will sabotage themselves without even realising they're doing it, and here's how it works...

Your brain, at its very basic level has two parts, your conscious mind and your unconscious mind. Now your conscious mind can concentrate on seven things – plus or minus two – at any one time, while your unconscious mind, well, scientists still haven't worked out the exact figure but if you take the average of the different studies you're looking at about 7,000,000 (and to have this super-computer to back you up and help you achieve your ambitions is pretty impressive!) However, there is a down side to this and that is that the unconscious mind is as dumb as a dodo.

It works with just a few basic rules and one of them is that it doesn't understand negatives, so, when it's presented with something it has to understand, it must first create it in order to be able to process it. Take someone trying to lose weight for an example. They may be saying to themselves "I have to stop eating chocolate cake" but all their unconscious mind hears is "eating chocolate cake" so it immediately goes to work and feeds the conscious mind with rich images of chocolate cake.

In fact it's likely to have even worked away in the background to deduce where the nearest chocolate cake is located and what the best way of getting it is (remember it can do 7,000,000 things at once). In this scenario it's far better to concentrate on what you want to gain – say being healthy and slim – than what you want to lose, because then the unconscious will feed you more helpful images and help you work out how to achieve your positive goal.

Another example is – and for any parents out there, I can absolutely guarantee you've done this or heard other parents doing it at least once – a child is climbing along a wall and the parent shouts "watch you don't fall". What does the child's unconscious mind hear? "Fall!" And it works out the best way to achieve this, runs rich images of it happening, and more times than not, helpfully follows through. Basically, it's imperative that you concentrate on what you want, and not on what you want to avoid.

Another statistic that I found really interesting is that 77% of self-talk is negative (you know, the little voice in your head that you have conversations with – and if you're sitting there thinking "I don't have a little voice in my head", that's it right there). If you're anything like me, you would never talk to someone else how you sometimes talk to yourself, so it's important to recognise what you're actually saying and how true that really is. To demonstrate this I'd like you to do a little exercise…

I'll describe a scenario to you and I want you to close your eyes and actually go through what I've described in rich detail. Ready?... Imagine that you're standing in your kitchen, it's a lovely warm day and sunlight is streaming through the window. You see that on one of the kitchen surfaces is a lemon, a chopping board and a knife. You walk over and pick up the lemon, feeling it in your hand. It's cool, smooth and you can feel the slight pimples in the skin.

You sniff it and there's a light citrus smell. You place it onto the chopping board pick up the knife and cut the lemon in half, and as you do so, some of the lemon juice runs out and you smell the clean, sharp tang. You take one of the halves of the lemon and cut that in two, then you pick up one of the quarters, hold it up to your nose, and smell the sharp, bitter and fresh tang. Now, bite deeply into the lemon… Run through the exercise and no cheating ☺

What happened? Your mouth watered didn't it. And that's mad when you really think about it. Without wanting to go all *The Matrix* on you, there is no lemon, and yet you had a physical reaction to something that quite simply didn't exist. It evidences perfectly how your brain doesn't know the difference between what you simply think and what you actually experience, so if you imagine negative things or say negative things to and about yourself, your brain takes them as absolute fact even though it might actually be rubbish (and is most of the time).

Why not make a note of any negative thoughts you're focusing on. Gather together a rough list and take just a moment to review it. A lot of the time, once you can actually see your thoughts for what they are, you can see just how ridiculous and harsh they can be. Why not try and replace them with positive affirmations, which are statements that make you feel good, or instead state goals you'd like to achieve.

Right in front of me now, for example, is a note saying 'I am an Amazon #1 bestselling author'. Now, I'm actually slightly dyslexic and sometimes my spelling is so bad that even my computer's spellchecker, whose sole job is to suggest correct replacement spellings, just flashes blankly at me with not a clue what I mean, so my brain could actually focus on a whole host of reasons why this could never be.

It could call me out and tell me that I'm a liar because, right at this second, it isn't actually true. But, having really looked at some of the negative stuff I've said to myself in the past, I've decided that they were lies too, so if I'm going to lie to myself, it might as well be a good one!

The reason it's so important to start with these affirmations and watch the way that we think is because our brains have to delete, distort and generalise the world in which we live in order to cope with so much information pouring in from the outside world. To see what I mean, right this second, take a moment to concentrate on your left foot. Is there any pressure on it? Can you feel material touching it? How warm or cool is it? Now, all of those sensations and feelings have always been there but you didn't notice before because your brain decided they weren't important and filtered them out.

These filters are shaped by the way that we see the world, and – as is our way – we get stuck into certain habits and so see certain things. It's undeniably true that what you concentrate on, you'll find more of. If you think that everyone's out to get you, for example, then your brain will find evidence of that to back up your thoughts. Or if you're looking for evidence that you're super-lucky, you'll find that too.

Depending on what you're filtering, you'll have a completely different experience of what's going on right now that the person sitting next to you. If you believe that it's really difficult to get new business, guess what, your brain will find loads of evidence to support that for you. How often have you been to the same party as someone else and you had an awesome time and thought it was the best ever, while they complained about the volume of the music, the poor food, or the rubbish company.

Whenever I sit down with a business owner for coaching, I always start with the end in mind. Their 'why'. Not long ago I was chatting with one new client about where they wanted to be in five years and they were struggling a bit to answer as they'd never sat down and really thought about it before. To help, I started to ask specific questions to prompt their thinking process, and one of them was 'how much holiday time would you like to be taking'. They considered it then replied "I'd love to be able to take a week's holiday". I won't print my exact response, but a sanitised version is along the lines of "are you crazy?" Can you imagine what would have happened had they continued with that line of thinking? Programming this super-computer with the thought that they would like a week's holiday in five years' time. More than likely, that's what they would've got and they'd then have been wondering, why, when they've worked so hard they can only get a week long holiday after five years.

During the recession in the 1990s there was an insurance company on the east coast of America and, like most businesses they'd been hit hard and were struggling. One day, the owner came into work, looked around the office and noticed, not surprisingly, that the sales people were flat, the atmosphere was glum, and that it just wasn't a great place to be.

But he then had an epiphany. Even if these were good times, even if there was no recession, they would have practically zero business coming in because of everyone's attitude. And he went on to think that if his guys were like this, then the competition must be similar, which meant that no-one was out there actually selling to potential clients.

What he did then was to get the sales people in to sit down with him one at a time and he asked them to set some personal goals that they'd like to achieve financially – whether that was getting a new car, going on a great holiday, or making home improvements – he got them to concentrate on these positives. He went on to explain that the competition wasn't out there selling, so there was a huge opportunity for them to grab loads of businesses, and with the exception of one guy (who soon left) everyone was on board. And guess what? The company doubled its turnover, during a recession, and attributed the whole growth to simply thinking differently about their circumstances and concentrating on positives.

You should by now have a bit of an understanding as to why it's important to have an end goal in mind, and how important it is to get your brain on side. So, the second 'why' I'd like to cover is your business 'why'. Why that business? And what impact are you trying to have on your clients?

There's a brilliant TED talk by Simon Sinek called "Why Great Leaders Inspire Action". If you've never seen TED it's a great resource of snappy 20 or so minute talks about pretty much any inspiring and educational topics you can think of. Their tag line is "ideas worth spreading" and it's definitely worth a look no matter what your interests are.

Simon Sinek talks about the Golden Circle:

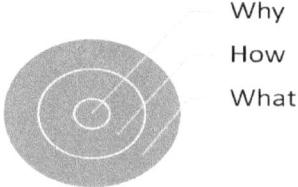

On the outside you have 'what you do', then 'how you do it', and finally 'why you do it' which is your core purpose or belief as a business. Simon explained that all really-inspired companies work from the inside out, rather than the traditional model where they work from the outside in, and he gave Apple as a great example.

If Apple was to market itself in the traditional way it would start with its 'what it does' which would focus on how "we make great computers", then their how, so, "we make computers that are user-friendly, beautifully-designed and easy to use, want to buy one?" Now, what Apple actually does is start with the 'why', so their marketing message sounds more like "everything we do, we believe in challenging the status quo, we believe in thinking differently" before they move into the 'how', "the way we challenge the status quo is everything we do is user-friendly, beautifully-designed, and easy to use", and then finally moving on to the what which is "we just happen to make great computers, want to buy one?".

He makes the point that people don't buy 'what' you do but 'why' you do it and Jim Collins, the renowned author of *Good to Great*, *Great by Choice* and *Built to Last* made a similar point. He studied some of the top companies in the world and compared them to similar businesses within their respective marketplace, who had the same opportunities, but who failed to thrive, do as well, or who – in some cases – actually went out of business.

Jim found that all of the companies that did exceptionally well had a clear vision of what they were doing (their why) a mission statement, and a really strong culture that all of the staff and customers (even if they didn't fully understand it) took on what they were trying to achieve.

Now, I'm not saying that you have to be building a £multi-million company, but what I am saying is that people buy people, so knowing your 'why' will help your potential customers chose to buy from you. If you're a builder for example, you could say "I build extensions" but isn't it better to somehow express what it is that you actually do for your customers, so something like "we create better environments for families to live, work and play in, and we do this by creating bespoke low maintenance extensions using quality materials and highly-skilled tradespeople. Want to buy one?"

So have a think about what your business 'why' is and really start to connect with the people involved.

---

**Chapter Summary**

- Why are you doing this? What's in it for you?

- Focus on the positives and get your unconscious mind on your side

- The importance of knowing your business why.

---

# CHAPTER 3

## Foundations for Your Business

M any years ago I started my career as an engineer and joined the Royal Navy at 18. It was the mid-1980s and the Cold War was in full swing, but I volunteered for the Submarine Service for two reasons. Firstly, they paid an extra £200 a month which – in the spirit of George Best – as a young guy meant an extra £180 a month for beer and women, and the rest, I could just waste ☺. Secondly, everything we did was a little bit more dangerous and super-secret (I could probably write a book about that too). I actually recently visited Portsmouth and toured some of the submariner museums and was a little gutted to see them packed full of stuff I use to work on – I mean I'm not even dead yet!

Anyway, the reason I brought up the engineering is because I learnt early on to always break things down to a process. At a very base level you have an input, something happens in the middle, and then there is an output. For business owners and entrepreneurs you normally have someone who is really good at what they do (input) and they want to be really successful (output) but then you have all of the stuff in the middle, which is where it seems to fall down.

The 'bit in the middle' is the same for anything that has any input or output, and if you want to reach the success that you crave, there's no getting away from the fact that it's going to take focus, it's going to take learning, and it's going to take investment in your business and most importantly in yourself. (Well done by the way for taking another step in investing in yourself with this book.)

When you look at people and how much they invest in their clothes, gym membership, cars, furnishings, TV or movies, holidays, and simply going out it's pretty staggering. And all so that their output is that they look good and keep themselves entertained. The greatest investment you can make though is in the six inches between your ears. If you lost everything in your life – your money, your house, cars, everything – the one thing you're unlikely to lose is what you've learnt and you can use this to rebuild yourself and craft a new life.

Jim Rohn once said "formal education will earn you a living, self education will make you a fortune". And don't be under any illusions that any people make this journey on their own. Take the example of Sir Clive Woodward who became the first full-time professional coach for the England Rugby Union team in 1997. Before coming into the job he had set up a successful computer-leasing company that made him a millionaire, and he used lots of the lessons he learned in business to coach the national side.

He understood the power of people and set about pulling together a vast and dynamic backroom team covering every discipline, to assist these top-of-their-game players to achieve more, and it was this expert coaching along with exacting discipline and an incredible work ethic that helped him achieve his number one goal – for England to be the best team in the world – at Sydney's Telstra Stadium on Saturday, 22 November, 2003.

But how do you get to that world cup-winning point? How do you work out where you're going right and where you may need to do a little more work? Well, take the way a maintenance engineer would fault-find as an example. With any piece of machinery they would look at the process and go to the half-way point to check whether everything was OK. If it was they'd look at the next halfway point, and so on until they find the issue, whereupon the process of fixing it can start. What I find with many businesses is the problem is at the very start of the process, which explains why so many are struggling.

Without devising a detailed working plan which gives the business the foundation to build upon, and the focus to work on what's important, success is more of a challenge than ever. Now I can already hear you saying "I'm hugely busy, I don't have time for anything else" and you're right. But just consider that for each one minute of planning you save yourself at least ten minutes of work. Plus, the only way you'll ever free up the time to plan is to take control. Don't worry, I'm here to help you claim back more of your time...

---

**Chapter Summary**

- Look at ways you can invest in yourself

- Look for people who can help you

- Fault-find like an engineer.

---

# CHAPTER 4

## Managing Yourself

I'm sure by this point you're thinking "well, all this stuff is great. I flicked through the content and I feel like this could be the beginning of something brilliant. If I could do this it would revolutionise my business…"

"But when do I have the time to do any of it? I'm flat out 12 hours a day just trying to keep things running smoothly in the business, then I have all of my family commitments, plus a list as long as my arm of stuff I want to do and stuff I'll have to do. Then you want me to implement all of these additional things into my business! Where am I supposed to find the time? I don't sleep enough as it is…"

And if you are thinking that – or anything like it – then please don't worry, you really are in the majority of business owners and entrepreneurs. I deliberately chose to include this chapter so early on in the book because if we can simply squeeze an additional 60 minutes out of your day, that would give you around an additional 45 working days a year. That's over a month that you don't currently have! And I do believe that if you really nail this, you'll be far more efficient and have a lot more time to play with than that.

This topic is typically referred to as 'time management', which when you think about it is a bit of a strange title. Everyone knows what you mean by time management, and you may have even paid to go on a time management course – I've run them myself – but let me share a secret… There's actually no such thing as managing time. (I usually save that nugget for my delegates after they've shown up!) After all, you can't store time. Everyone has all the time there is. Nobody has more time than you in a day. Increased demand does not mean increased supply. And it's not flexible (ignoring Einstein's Theory of Relativity, for a while at least). What it's actually all about is self-management, and you'll have particular challenges depending on your circumstance and what is allowed to distract you.

It might be that you procrastinate or avoid doing certain jobs – we all have distractions that can all-too-easily interfere with our day – but we simply need to make sure that we're in control. When you look, you might even notice certain emotional triggers that lead you astray. It's all about having that awareness of what's going on that will ultimately let you take control.

A few years ago, I had to write up a dissertation for my Neuro Linguistic Programming Masters that I'd been working on for five months. I had a mountain of research and videos that I had already gone through and I simply had to start the process of typing everything up. Now, to be honest I'm not the world's fastest typist and I actually felt a bit overwhelmed by how much work I had to do.

My house was lovely and clean, my urgent jobs were all done, the computer was on and I had my work laid out to the one side of me and a cup of tea for me to sip on the other. As I sat down at my desk, the sun was streaming in through the patio window, and I was well and truly ready to start. But then I looked up and saw the light fitting which was dangling down by the wire. I'd only bought the house six months earlier and this was one of the jobs I just hadn't gotten around to doing yet. So, what did I do? Yes, that's right, I went and got my tools and spent 45 minutes fixing it.

Now, when I sat back down I looked up at the light fitting and felt really good that I'd finally done it. But then I looked at the work and felt overwhelmed again. As the realisation that I was letting myself get hijacked into not starting the work I needed to do hit me, I smiled to myself, took a breath, and started to break down what I needed to do into smaller tasks, making it all less daunting and much easier to get started. Now I'm also more aware of my emotional responses to certain jobs, and I have my own tactics for dealing with them.

So, looking at the story above as an example, how do you 'eat an elephant' or deal with any large project? Simply cut it up into smaller pieces, prioritise the actions to be taken, and then create an action list and – one bite at a time – you'll slowly move forwards until the elephant is gone and you've achieved your goal.

## Are You Addicted to Urgency?

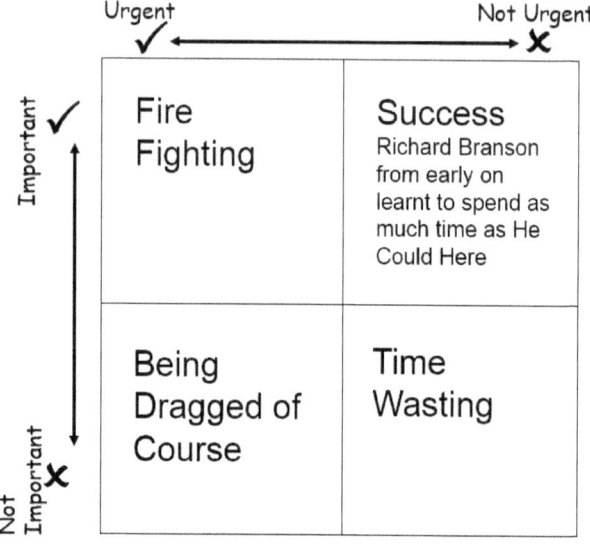

Looking at this chart, how much of what you do is in the ideal box of *not urgent but important*? That's success. The planning and information which is essential for building your business. It's OK to cross over to the *urgent and important* box sometimes: clients may need prompt help, situations you can't plan for may occur, or on occasion you may need to change your plans at the last minute. But many business owners actually spend most of their day dealing with *urgent but not important* tasks like emails and client calls, or even worse, *not urgent and not important* activities like social media.

Ultimately, one thing you do have to get good at is planning – that's the *important but not urgent* stuff – and this is where all the super-successful people spend the majority of their time. You need a daily, weekly, monthly, and yearly action list and it will soon become a habit. One of the things that I do which has really revolutionised how I work and play, is sitting down with my partner once a week and planning our week and what we'd like to achieve across all areas of our lives: work, career, money, home and family, health and fitness, and wellness.

We get down a white board that has our yearly and quarterly goals noted and we look at what we steps we want to take towards those bigger goals this week. To be honest, we don't always get everything done that we planned. Life gets in the way, we work late, or we're out at a function or seeing a client. We do always get lots of the stuff done though so, bit by bit, we're moving towards achieving our big goals, one bite of the elephant at a time.

A little bit later we're going to get you to write down what you want to achieve in the next five years, and then bring this forward to what you want to achieve in the next year. Once you've done this, why not break it down into the next three months, and then very specifically what you can do in the next week to move you towards your goals and desires. And while you may not achieve everything, by prioritising your top three goals that *must* be completed, and by keeping your goals somewhere you can see them daily, you'll take great strides towards achieving your dreams.

But how do you get more time to do all of this? Well firstly you need to understand where your time goes, and a great way to do this is to track what you do every day, in either 15 minute or 30 minute intervals. See what happens to your time and who or what is stealing it. Pinpoint your top 'time stealers' and then look at how you can manage them.

Try it now. Track your activity for a day, then write down your top time thives and look to see if you can delegate, eliminate or simplfly them.

I read an article recently that said that with such an array of social media available, including Twitter, Facebook, Pinterest, Google Plus, and YouTube – to name just a few – plus texts, phone calls, and people popping in or asking questions, the average person is interrupted once every 11 minutes. This is shocking enough, but when you consider that getting focused on what you're doing can take around 25 minutes, many of us spend our days without ever really being able to focus on anything that we're doing.

And now that the idea of being able to multi task and switch between jobs to do more things has been debunked, with recent studies showing that your IQ drops by ten points each time you try, compared to smoking marijuana which only sees it drop by five points, and you get a valuable comparison.

OK, so where should you begin? It all starts with a routine and blocking out your day so that you focus on whatever it is that you're doing with no distractions. Schedule to pick up your emails just twice a day – perhaps 10am till 11am, and 3pm till 4pm, then set aside a time to return calls – you may wish to do this once a day but limit it to a maximum of twice a day regardless. Then schedule in the rest of the stuff you need to do around this.

Take some time on a Sunday night to write out your perfect week ahead.

This may give you a rough guide of what you are trying to achieve:

Alan S Adams Helping You To Thrive
www.alansadams.com

You may be thinking "I can't do that, my customers expect to be able to get hold of me" but just consider for a moment that unless you're a member of the emergency services or urgent response, it's highly unlikely that it's a genuine life or death situation. Plus, if your customers expect instant feedback, stop for a moment and ask yourself who's trained them to think that way…

Has anyone ever emailed you to say 'the building's on fire'? And how many issues need you to instantly respond on the phone? As long as you revert back to the client on the same day, or even within a few hours, it shouldn't be a problem. If it is, then set up an emergency email or have a dedicated line or mobile to deal with pressing issues (and if you can charge a premium rate for providing this, then make sure you do as it will make people think twice about using it).

And with every email you receive, make sure that you deal with it as you read it the first time. Ask yourself the following questions and take these actions:

1. Does it concern you? If no, pass it on
2. Do you need to keep it? If no, bin it
3. Is it useful? Yes, file or read it, no, bin it
4. Does it need action? Yes, do it or file it.

Create a routine and check emails at certain times of the day. Create files and systems for easy retrieval, and learn to scan and speed read them.

I don't often advocate using an answering machine to field and screen calls, as you risk potential customers hanging up without leaving a message, so why not consider using a professional telephone answering service? These are normally relatively low-cost, the staff are trained to answer the phone as you wish and take core information, then they email you details of the enquiry so that you can pick it up when it suits you better. And again, if it does require an immediate response, the call-handler can email an 'emergency' address where you can see and respond to it.

Another great way to seize control of your day is to decide on, and put into action, bookends for your day. You can't often control every element of the main portion of your day, but you can control what happens immediately after you wake up and just before you go to bed. You may decide to read a few pages of a positive book, to meditate or focus on your goals, or to spend a short period of time exercising. Perhaps you decide to listen to an audio book on your commute to work too. Activity first thing in your day is all about getting your brain into the right frame of mind and turning unproductive time into something positive.

Then, when you get into work, block off the first 60 minutes of your day to work on your business or an important project. Then and only then open your emails, answer the phone, return calls, or brief your team. If you have an office, put a Do Not Disturb sign on the door when you're working on one of your blocks of time. If you're in an open plan office, use some headphones and make sure that everyone knows not to disturb you. You'll quite often find that one particular time of the day is when you're most productive, so use that time to do whatever activity you get the highest return on investment from.

Nigel Botterill is a true entrepreneur and has built eight separate £million pound business. He uses this technique and he's so protective of his first 90 minutes in the morning that he has a "Do Not Disturb Unless There's A Fire" sign on his door. His team know that interrupting Nigel during this time is potentially a disciplinary issue, because those 90 minutes of being able to work on his business each day are so precious and he knows they're absolutely critical to his future success.

I met another super successful guy a few years ago – Darren Hardy. His book, *The Compound Effect*, focuses on the little things you do every day and how these small actions and choices can compound to have a huge impact on your life and business in five years time. That may be negative, such as a few biscuits a day leading to a big weight gain over time, or positive in terms of reading a few pages of a book leading to significant learning and development. I think that Nigel's 90 minute habit is a brillant demonstration of this very subject. Of how small actions done consistently every day start to compound into big impacts.

At the end of your day you may decide to look back at what you've accomplished, perhaps note a few things down in a gratitude or acknowledgment list. You may read a few pages of a good book, do some yoga or stretching, and write your To Do list for the next day so that you can hit the ground running. The choice is absolutely yours, but these bookends need to become a core part of your day, non-negotiable, and completed whatever else is going on.

After all, if the first thing you do in the morning is open your emails then you're instantly allowing your day to be hijacked by other people – you're immediately marching to the beat of someone else's drum and you may never seize back control. Do your bookends and you can rest assured that you're regularly doing something that is moving you forward towards your goals, no matter what else happens during the day.

Now, it's no good starting and ending your day well, and blocking out parts of your day for core activities if you then have distractions popping up constantly. So, switch off your email alert, you know, that little box that pops up telling you an email has just arrived. No email should ever be so urgent that it has to be dealt with immediately.

Then switch your phone on to silent and remove the vibrate function (and this includes alerts for emails, messages, calls, and all of your social media channels). You can check for messages every 90 minutes if you have to, and can schedule a call-back or response at the time you've allocated. To help you manage these interruptions, remember that they're taking you away from what you *need* to do, and so taking time away from what you *want* to do. Follow my five points below and start to free yourself:

1. Outsource incoming telephone calls and message-taking
2. Avoid small talk
3. Be assertive – it's OK to say no
4. Prioritise the interruption – how important is it really?
5. Develop effective telephone skills.

Also, look to delegate or outsource as many tasks as possible from the list you made earlier. It's likely that your time is worth a minimum of £50 per hour, so why would you do a job that you could get someone else to do for less? You shouldn't be doing your own bookkeeping even if you're good at it or you enjoy doing it, and other tasks like data entry or administration are absolutely essential for the smooth running of your operations but also don't need to be done by you.

If – like many people – you struggle to let go of certain jobs because you believe that no one else can do it as well as you, ask yourself "if my business was turning over £1,000,000, would I be doing this job?". Or, if you struggle with that one, ask "if Richard Branson was running my business would he be doing this?" And if the answer is "no" find a way to delegate it to someone else, outsource it, or create a system to take care of it.

Think about the skills that you need to run your business efficiently and think about your function and role. What actions or activity gets left and becomes urgent and important? What are routine tasks, and what falls under the banner of administration? Then coach and train your team so that you can let go, and outsource whatever else you can.

Meetings have often been considered the practical alternative to work, and managing your meetings effectively is crucial in allowing you to take back control of your day. Meetings can be just the biggest waste of time when attendees get stuck on the smallest detail and can't or won't move forward. One tip I picked up from Johnny, in between him telling me stories, is to focus on the minutes from the last meeting at the end, as you often find that many of the points have already been covered and you can whizz through them. Consider these tips when planning and taking part in meetings in the future:

1. Think about the meeting format. Does it need to be face-to-face or can it be done via some other medium like Skype?
2. They should all have a set purpose and objective, and all attendees should be clear on what this is

3. Set an appropriate time to start and to finish the meeting and agree it. Then stick to it
4. Set, prioritise and circulate an agenda before the meeting
5. Make sure that you cover important items first, that way if you run out of time the core topics have been covered even if you don't discuss everything.

With your time management and allocation do also remember that it's not all about work, you have to look after yourself and your emotional well-being too. All too often we can feel overwhelmed by life and what we have to do, and that's not just within the workplace. We can worry about the mountain of tasks we have to do and can just end up procrastinating or being really busy and achieving very little of what's most important in driving our businesses or lives forward.

Being in control, or should I say feeling that you're in control, is critical to your productivity, happiness and – as it turns out – your health. A 1997 landmark study conducted of 7,400 employees showed that those who believed they had no control over deadlines that had been set were 50% more likely to suffer with coronary disease, and that's as high a health concern as having high blood pressure!

In another study, a selected group of older people living full-time in a residential care home were giving the task of looking after their own plants. This small responsibility and sense of control within their lives not only made them feel happier but it actually reduced mortality rates when compared with others in the same home who didn't look after their own plants and simply watched staff take on the task. Such is the importance of feeling in control that it can even prolong life.

OK, so now for another quick exercise. Take a piece of paper and turn it so that it's horizontal, then draw a line down the middle, and on the left hand side list the things that are worrying you but that you have no direct influence over. On the right hand side write down the things that are worrying you but that you do have influence over and so are able to control to some degree.

Now cross out the things that you've acknowledged that you can't control. Forget about them – there's nothing that you can do to influence or impact on them, so move on and instead concentrate on what you *can* control. You may not be able to control whether a client leaves you for example, but you can control putting extra effort into developing your products or skill-set to provide added value to them. Prioritise your list and select a couple of things that you can take action on, even if they're tiny to start with.

Ultimately, if we can manage our distractions and take back control over how we spend our time, we can become far more efficient at what we're doing. But – and here's the fly in the ointment – if what we're doing isn't following the right strategy in the first place, we still won't be getting anywhere, we'll just be a lot more efficient at not getting there. Don't worry though, we'll cover strategy soon and make sure that you're on the right path.

Here are a few other things to consider for your own wellbeing at the moment:

1. If you're stuck on a piece of work, struggling for a killer idea, or can't quite word something for that important proposal, take some time away to do something else
2. Keep fit and focus on your health – you need a strong body and lots of energy to be at your best
3. Leave work in the office and make a mental divide between work time and home time
4. Take breaks away from where you work
5. Manage your negative self-talk, change "should" to "could" which acknowledges that you have a choice, and recognise that no one is perfect – just think how you'd react if someone else spoke to you as you speak to yourself
6. Focus on positive affirmations
7. Make time to see and stay in touch with friends and family – they're important.

So, now this is where you go back to the Ideal Week Planner you did earlier and plan in where all of these activities are going to take place. As far as possible these should be set in stone, as it's these activities that will ultimately get you to where you want to be. I know it seems like extra work, but I promise you that doing this will put you in the top few % of business owners in the country. But don't be fooled. A lot of these activities may not yield results for months or even years, but consistently doing them will eventually allow you to catch momentum and then you really are going to start to shift.

**Chapter Summary**

- Discover your time thieves

- Create your Perfect Week

- Create your perfect bookends

- Manage your distractions

- Work on what's important every day.

# CHAPTER 5

## Where's The Money?

How many times has your accountant shown you great-looking spreadsheets which show a positive profit. And how many times have you thought about the cash currently sat in your bank and wondered where exactly that money has gone? The thing is, profits do not equal cash in the bank, and your 'money' is actually tied up in a variety of places. The sum that you should be working to is:

cash
> \+ stock
> \+ work in progress
> \+ accounts receivable
> – accounts payable
> = Profit

All too often I see business owners not putting things in place to maximise the cash that they have in the bank, and if this rings true with you too, then let's look and see if we can get some quick wins...

Depending on the industry that you're in, stock carried can be huge and can act as a massive drain on your resources – not just in terms of the money it ties up but also the space it uses. I heard a story recently about a company that hadn't really ever looked properly at what their stock levels were or what they were actually holding.

The guy running the stock room was an ex-engineer and as they were delivering mainly engine parts when they set up 25 years previously he'd seemed like the natural choice for the job. When a consultant came in and posed the question of stock levels, they started to take a look at what they were actually holding for the first time and were horrified. They had over £300,000 worth of stock and a lot of it was more than 20 years old so now obsolete. Now this wasn't an enormous company that had £300,000 to spare. The company started to list a lot of the stuff on eBay just to get rid of it and free up space as well as get some of their cash back.

Don't fall into this trap, take a look at what you hold in stock and review if it's sufficient and appropriate. Is there a better way of doing things? Can you hold slightly less, or get rid of some stock altogether? Could you change your model to drop-shipping where you don't hold stock at all and a third party manages all of your fulfilment? Or could you organise a deal where you're supplied with stock within 24 hours of ordering? After all, there's a reason that many of our leading manufacturing and engineering companies work on 'just in time' contracts with their suppliers.

Work in progress is anything that you've received an order for but that you've not yet invoiced. Within any industry it's imperative that you get the flow of work as efficient as possible, so that the work gets completed quickly and so that the invoice gets sent as soon as possible. Doing the invoicing every other week or once a month simply isn't good enough, as it can add weeks onto the time before the cash for the job hits your account.

I even heard someone once say that they "were too busy to invoice" which is just madness! Why else are we in business? And do factor in too that the longer you take to invoice, the less likely your customer is to pay. Numerous studies have shown that if someone hasn't paid you within 90 days, the likelihood of them actually doing so drops dramatically, so make sure that you have strong and robust processes in place.

Consider trying to get clients on direct debits or standing orders, and perhaps offer incentives for them to do so by way of added value or better terms. Also, ensure you have a robust follow-up system to politely remind your clients when it's due seven days before the due date. A lot of small business owners are really busy themselves and appreciate the reminder. Also, don't let clients run over by more than 45 days unless you have rock solid reasons. There are all sorts of services out there to help you chase payment, just choose the most appropriate for you and your needs.

Writing this has just reminded me of a classic example of the importance of invoicing… About five years ago I used a garage to get the cam belt in one of our cars changed and when I went to pay the owner said he hadn't done the invoice yet and he'd give me a shout. He never did get in touch and I've only just remembered. I'm not even sure they're still trading and I wonder why?

The flow of your work is absolutely critical so try to step back from what you do and actually look at the different steps that it takes to complete a job. Think about how your product is physically moved around, or your service is provided. Look at who's controlling it and what the time limits on jobs are and whether they're being kept to.

You'll often find one member of your team asking another to do a five minute job for them, which distracts them from what they've been allocated. This can cause massive inefficiency within the flow of jobs, and in this scenario you have to make sure one person is in charge of each job, otherwise efficiency just goes out of the window.

Consider using timesheets to see who's doing what, and make sure that your team understand the importance of moving straight onto the next job when they finish the previous one. This in itself can be an issue in some industries, take creatives and graphic designers for example. They may be allocated six hours to do a job, may manage to finish it in four hours but then may spend the last two hours trying to improve slight details that nobody will notice. Those two hours could have been used to work on something else, and if they do that every time and you're looking at around four months a year spent doing stuff that no one will actually notice.

Every industry is different of course, but it's absolutely critical to get your money in as soon as possible. Consider asking people to make upfront payments. As a coach this is something I've always done, but I also give a 500% - return on investment and money-back guarantee for peace of mind. If you have clients on retainers there's an opportunity to flip your cash flow, especially with new clients who are coming on board and I've done this with a few. But what's one of the most effective ways to increase cash flow? Put up your prices!

And yet price increases strike fear into the hearts of most business owners, so they simply don't do it. But this irrational fear is keeping people working long hours for what is often not a great amount of money. This reminds me of a story about Jill. Now Jill had a jewellery shop and also had an e-commerce site to sell the jewellery. She had a lot of stock in one type of jewellery that just hadn't shifted, so she decided to just take the hit to get rid of it by having a half-price sale online. She was going to contact her database of customers to let them know, left instructions for the member of staff that deals with the online side of the business, and went away for a few days. When she came back, she was pleased to see that virtually all of the stock had gone, then gobsmacked that the member of staff hadn't seen ½ price sale, she'd just seen the 2 so had doubled the price of all the items. The customers' perception was that these were quality items and worth the price, so they bought them. Her problem was well and truly solved.

In your business always have an awareness of who you're selling to and what their expectations are. Also, if you know any tradesmen, ask them whether they've ever increased the price of a job because they didn't want it, only to have the customer come back and engage them. In a lot of cases you'll find, they have, in fact one guy I know actually doubled the price and the customer still came back to say yes.

Do you understand your numbers? If your margins are 10%, for example, and you put your prices up by 10% , what percentage of your customers could you afford to lose? Believe it or not it's actually half of them! And to prove it just look at this example:

> You buy at 9, sell at 10, you sell 10, and you've made 10
> You buy at 9, sell at 11, you sell 5, and you've made 10

So, you've made the same money with half the effort. I know that these may not be your numbers, but you have to understand what's going on within your business and you have to stop making excuses for not adjusting your price up as you need. One of the questions I ask when speaking to a group of business owners is "who here charges, roughly speaking, average prices for their product or services?" Normally more than half of the room will raise their hands. Then I ask "who here delivers average services or product?" Typically, very few put their hand up. And what does that tell us?...

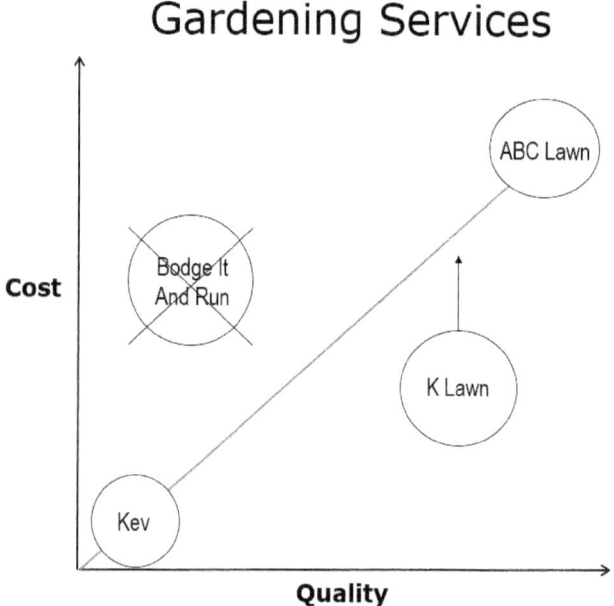

Now it's time for a really easy exercise to help you understand exactly where you sit within your market. It's one I use quite often to help clients overcome their fear of price rises, and you'll notice on the example above we have *price* verses *quality* on the axes. On the graph itself you have a 'value for money' line smack bang centre, and in our example we've used imaginary lawn cutting services here, just to give you a feel of how it all works. ABC Lawns, is high cost but high value, While Kev – who is still on the value-for-money line – is low cost and low value. You don't want to be where Bodge it and Run are as that's a recipe for bankrupty. Now K Lawn is actually well below the value for money line and can put up their prices by quite a bit.

I can't tell you the amount of times I do this with business owners and entrepreneurs who I'm advising to put their prices up, but who – even with a price rise – are still well below the 'ideal' value for money line with a better quality product than the competition. And usually the competition is charging more. It's shocking.

Now, after saying how important it is for you to get your money as quickly as possible, I'm now going to say that you shouldn't pay your suppliers too quickly. I'm not advocating holding payment or making late payments, but many small businesses will pay a bill as soon as they get the invoice, which is all well and good, but if the payment terms are 30 days then you could hold that cash in your account until the due date as it can help your own cashflow no end. Remember the old business saying: "Turnover is insanity, profit is sanity, **but cash, cash is king"**.

**Chapter Summary**

- Know your margins

- Understand the flow of work and see if you can make it more efficient

- Know where your cash is in your business

- Put up your prices.

# CHAPTER 6

## There's No Silver Bullet

Now You'll sometimes hear people saying "if only this would happen" or "if only we could get that we'd be made". Well, I hate to tell you but in my experience there is no silver bullet within business. No "if only", and no "one answer or action to building a great business". It's about small changes across every area of the business, so let's look at these and give you a worked example...

What we're going to look at is how focusing specifically on each area of our business in turn can show potentially huge opportunities to increase turnover:

First we have the number of **customers** that are currently purchasing of you, this is anyone who is coming back to within the purchasing cycle of your goods or services, but you also have to think about anyone that has ever bought from you. If you've been going for a while you're going to have people's details somewhere. Do you have a database? If not, perhaps you could look at old invoices to secure this information and you could then transfer it onto a database as that will allow you to get in touch again.

Trust me, this is one area you really don't want to fall down on, as your financial future depends on having up-to-date details for anyone that you've ever come into contact with. And when I say anyone, I mean everyone. So, if they've phoned you, browsed your website, walked through your door, asked for information, bought from you online, or every caught your attention, you need to capture their details. Bear in mind legal and best practice guidance of course though, and always give people the opportunity to unsubscribe from any communications.

And do remember that an average 68% of your clients leave because of perceived indifference in that they simply don't think you care. So, whatever you do, make sure they feel the love no matter how long it takes them to come back.

**New Leads** is any potential new business that comes your way via whatever marketing methods you're focusing on. It could be emails, phone calls, quotes, referrals, or people simply walking through your door. And just going back to the database, do your absolute best to capture these potential customers' details and put them on to your database.

**Converting New Leads** is the actual percentage of new clients that you get to hand over money and become one of your lucky new customers.

**Average Number of Purchases Each Year** is how often your clients return to you.

And **the Average Value of Each Purchase** is the total value of your sales divided by the total number of your customers, to give you an average spend.

OK, so looking at these figures what we're going to do is increase each one by 10%. Not a huge number by any stretch, and using the tactics we talk about later in the book you should be able to do this easily in your business

– in fact when you stop to think, it's simply small steps like getting your conversion ratio from 25% to 27.5%, so we're really not asking too much.

| | | |
|---|---|---|
| **Customers** | **120** | **140** |
| **New Leads** | **80** | **88** |
| **Converting Leads** | **25%** | **27.5%** |
| **Total Customer Now** | **140** | **164.2** |
| **Average Purchases PA** | **9.3** | **10.2** |
| **Purchase Average Value** | **£375** | **£412.50** |
| **TOTAL SALES** | **£488,250** | **£690,030** |

As you can see here, the small changes noted in the right hand column – across the whole business – result in an increase of £201,780 or a 41% uplift in sales! How cool is that ☺

---

**Chapter Summary**

- Small changes across your business will reap huge rewards – work through the example and see your business's positive potential.

---

# CHAPTER 7

## What's Guiding You?

What is it you're really looking to achieve? What's the purpose of your business?

Your vision and mission for the business, and the culture that you're looking to develop or maintain, needs to be written down for everyone involved with your business to see.

In *Delivering Happiness* Tony Hsieh shares the story of how he sold his first company for $250,000,000. He tells how in the early days he was excited to go into work, he loved the people he was working with, and was having a great time. In the early days he was offered $2,000,000 for the company but held onto it, not because the two million wasn't a lot of money, but because he loved what he was doing. However, as the company grew, Tony lost the joy and eventually – just before he sold the company – he really had to drag himself into work. At first he struggled to understand why he felt like that, but when he was in work one day and looking around, he realised that the place just felt a lot different – it had grown quickly and the new people coming into the business had different attitudes and ways of doing things.

The business that Tony loved had now developed a culture and values of its own and they were at odds with what Tony and his partners had first set up. And this meant that he no longer felt like he belonged there, nor did he want to be there. So, Tony promised himself that the next business that he was involved with would not suffer the same issues. And when he did get involved with Zappos, he worked with his team to develop a collaborative written vision, mission, and values for the company. Anyone coming into the business was shown these and it was made clear that they had to fully engage with the company's culture.

Now this is powerful stuff and I can wholeheartedly recommend that you consider it in your business if you don't have it already. It's been well documented that if people verbalise a belief, even if it's one that they didn't hold before, they are much more likely to act as if that belief is real. Even if you're sitting there thinking "my business has already developed a culture that I don't like" you have the power to change it.

A brilliant example of this is Seattle's *Pike Place Fish Market* which is now world-famous. Read the short book *Fish* by Stephen C. Lundin, Harry Paul and John Christensen to learn more about how they achieved the culture they did, but it's a wildly successful, fun, and bustling place, with a joyful atmosphere and fantastic customer service. The team literally throw fish from one side of the market to the other, and they get crowds of people coming down to see the action and even get involved. However, it wasn't always that way, it used to be just a job to the employees and not a great one as it was often cold and smelly.

But they all came together one day and decided that if they were going to come to work every day they might as well be the best, and have fun doing it. Through a process of trial and error, they learnt by applying ingeniously-simple lessons which allowed them to become *The World Famous Pike Place* – and it's interesting to note that they actually called themselves 'world famous' long before they actually were (remember what we were talking about earlier about beliefs...) They now have lots of fun, and you can do the same to energise and transform your workplace if you choose to.

Some other great examples of strong and positive cultures are places like Apple, Google, and Innocent. Even their offices are pretty extraordinary. During a recent trip to Innocent's Head Office in London I had the chance to have a good chat with Richard Reed, one of the co-founders. He's a really nice, genuine guy and you get the feeling that the company operates that way too. He tells the story about how they actually got started as a business by taking a stand at a music festival and placing two bins in front of their stand: one with 'yes' and the other with 'no' written on. They asked everyone who bought their drinks "should we quit our jobs and set up in business making these full-time" and all committed to following the consensus opinion. At the end of the weekend, the "yes" bin was full, so the next day they did indeed all quit their jobs and started Innocent full-time.

If you've never seen their products or the way that they market themselves, do take the time to check them out – they're an example of brilliance and their culture and personality shines through everything. Rather than a use-by date, for example, they have an "enjoy by" date. And they actually went through a phase of not only having the ingredients on the bottles but putting some fun stuff on too – most famously, "two plump nuns", which ended with Richard being taken to court by trading standards. A few weeks after the appearance, he tells how he received a letter from the judge saying that he "needed to either remove the two plump nuns reference from the ingredients label or start adding them to the product" ☺

On their packaging they also advise customers to ring the 'customer service banana phone' and – if you get the chance to take one of the tours they offer – you'll see this in pride of place. Most interesting though, they have their culture and mission statements clearly and proudly displayed on the walls for everyone to see.

**Their vision statement is:** Make natural, delicious food and drink that helps people live well and die old.

**And their mission statement is:** Everything innocent makes will always be 100% natural, delicious and nutritionally net-positive, so people are physically and mentally better off after they have eaten our food than before. In other words, we want to be a Trojan horse in society, getting as much fruit and vegetables into people as possible, to help us all live well and die old.

**Their culture is set out as:**

**Be Natural**
Not just our products, but being natural in how we treat each other and how we speak to the most important people – our drinkers.

**Be Entrepreneurial**
Innocent began as a small, entrepreneurial company, and nothing much has changed. We aren't afraid to do things differently, and we've never given up on a good opportunity.

**Be Responsible**
We keep our promises, are mindful of our impact on our community and our environment, and always try to leave things a little bit better than we found them.

**Be Commercial**
We wouldn't be here if we didn't keep our eyes on the numbers at all times. Ultimately we want to deliver growth for us and our customers too.

**Be Generous**
This means giving honest feedback to one another, taking time to say thank you, and where we can, donating our resources or money to those who need it more than us. It's that simple.

Talking to the staff there they clearly love where they work, and even admitted that they could work somewhere else for more money but simply didn't want to. They enjoy what they're a part of creating. Just imagine if you could harness that passion in your business.

To develop your own vision, mission, and culture for your business, start by writing down lots of ideas. Don't put pressure on yourself, you're not likely to get it perfect first time, but keep coming back to it and writing some more and eventually you'll get something that you're happy with. To give you an idea of what other organisations have chosen, here are a few from some of the globally-best-known brands:

3M          To solve unsolved problems innovatively

Boeing      To push the leading edge of aviation,
            taking on huge challenges and doing what

|   |   |
|---|---|
|   | others cannot do |
| Merck | To preserve and improve human life |
| Nike | To experience the emotion of competition, winning, and crushing competitors |
| Teaching Co | To ignite in all people the passion for learning |
| Sony | To experience the sheer joy of advancing and applying technology for the benefit of the public |
| Walt Disney | To make people happy |
| Times Mirror | To contribute to the performance of the communities we serve |
| WL Gore | To have fun doing innovative things that make money |
| Wal-Mart | To give ordinary folk the chance to buy the same things as rich people. |

Now write down what your mission statement is and then your business's culture. Look at your culture and what you're trying to achieve. Once you have people coming into your business, you need to tell them what to expect. Also, if you lay it out at the start, they're much more likely to follow it and don't forget that if you don't lay out the culture, the business will develop one anyway and it might be one that isn't great.

**Chapter Summary**

- The importance of developing a Vision, Mission Statement and Culture.

# CHAPTER 8

## Building Your Marketing Plan

Marketing is often misunderstood and thought to be simply the leaflets or advertising that you do. It isn't. Marketing is everything from the product you decide to sell – whether that's a premier product or a cheap-as-chips product – to the way that you invoice, right through to the very culture of your business. All of this comes under the banner of marketing as it all affects how you're perceived by current and potential customers and your wider stakeholder community.

So, let's start by considering who your ideal client is? Where do they shop? What type of magazines do they read? Which papers do they subscribe to? Do they use any online services? Where do they live? What are their ages? Do they have a family? Where do they go on holiday? The better picture you can build up, the more targeted your marketing can be, and you can use this information to develop a couple of avatars of your ideal clients to enable you to better target them.

Within your marketplace, give some thought to what your product or service is. Who is your target market? What turnover do you need to generate to get you the profit and lifestyle you want? And what is the timescale for you building this?

You have to completely understand the marketplace you're in, so what are your key features and how do you compare to your competitors on market share,

quality and price? What are the main differences between you and your competitors? This will all give you a feel of how best to understand your position within the market. Also, do have an awareness of where your competitors are advertising, but don't make the mistake of assuming that you have to be there too.

There a great story about one of Nigel Botherill's first businesses which he started with his wife Sue. A business opportunity, they offered people a postcode area and all of the support that they needed to get a local magazine up and running. They earned from the advertising revenue, which – once up and running – could bring in reasonable returns for part-time hours.

Their big break came when Red magazine, whose circulation includes corporate mums who were potentially looking for a way out of the corporate world so they could spend more time with the children (one of their avatars), did an article on them. They were flooded with leads and women looking to take up this business opportunity. Nigel then continued to advertise with Red for reasonable returns, but none of his competitors ever did.

Now this is an example of how Public Relations (PR) can really work for your business, and I would actively encourage you to be proactive with PR and - if you can - engage with a great PR firm.

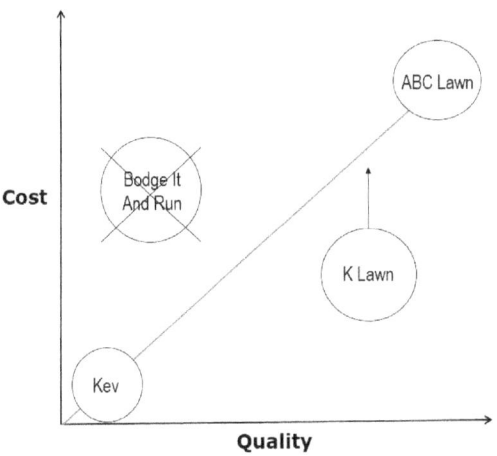

## Gardening Services

OK so thinking back to this diagram again, get a pen and paper and draw out how you compare against your competition. Where do you sit? If you're just below the line (so actually offering slightly higher value than you're charging) that's a great place to be, because you're delivering slightly more than your customers are paying for (only slightly mind, and make sure they understand the added value you're giving them).

You clearly you don't want to be where Bodge it and Run is, that's a proven recipe for disaster. Now, what this will do is give you a really good idea of where you are in the marketplace and it doesn't simply have to be *cost versus quality*, you could replace the titles on the axes with *cost versus number of services,* or *time versus quality...* In fact you can do a whole array of graphs to get a really good feel for where you sit and where your competition is.

This is worth reiterating because price is the one area where business owners have their biggest fear. I've found time and time again when I've done this, that businesses are charging too little for the service or product they are giving. Quite often this gives business owners a new perspective on what they do and what can be charged. After all if you're delivering a better product or service than your competitors and charging a lot less, whose fault is it?

Just a further note on putting up prices. If you put your prices up, on average you may lose roughly 15% of your customers (remember the example earlier though, you can afford to lose them) and if you contact your customers and position the price rise properly, you shouldn't lose any.

Here's something else I typically ask a room full of businesspeople when I have the opportunity. "Have you ever lost a deal based on price?" Normally a lot of the room put their hand up. Then I ask "have you ever won a deal based on price?" And here just a few put their hands up. Interesting... There is certainly something to be said about price. A few people will simply buy the cheapest no matter what, and believe me you don't want them as customers – there's no loyalty, they'll go somewhere else for a saving of £1 and in my experience they're the biggest pain, demanding more for their money and wanting more of your time than your clients that pay top fees.

Give some thought to what products make you the biggest profits. What type of clients pay you the most and take up the least amount of your time or involve the least effort to service. It's hugely important when developing your marketing plan that you know exactly what your best products are and how those are going to develop. Also, do remember, that it's not just about what pays you the most, after all the definition of a business is "a commercial profitable business that pays you whether you're there or not". I've built a residual income which in the early days didn't pay me a great deal when compared to my hourly rate, but which all these years later now pays me a significant sum every single month whether I ever work in it again or not. So do always keep the end goal in mind.

With your clients, consider whether you can set things up on retainers, or products on auto-ship, so that you reach your break-even point for running your business each month even before you start working on new business. And are there any other ways to get them to pay up front, or pay more up front if you're already doing this? I have one client who typically has both project and retained work. Now, funnily enough having mentioned price before, I had them double their prices during the first period I worked with them because they were worth it (and I still believe they could have gone a bit further). Anyway, they were keen to increase cash flow so I suggested they offer clients a 3 month pre-pay scheme where they received some additional complimentary work after 12 months.

To say the client was resistant to this idea was an understatement. They had lots of what they thought were valid arguments, Member of a Chartered Institution, not best practice, no one will want to do it, we can't afford to lose clients, it just won't work. You get the picture. Eventually they gave in and did it. The result? Not only did their clients love it, it flipped their cash flow and helped tie in their clients to longer term relationships without the need for a contract. Win, win and win!

I also saw a great example of a beauty salon where the owner selected all of her best customers, threw a VIP launch party that was invitation only, and offered the people there a special deal where they sign up to a retainer and receive £200 of beauty treatments a month for only £160. She had enough sign-ups that night to cover the main costs of running the business every single month before she even made another sale. What could you introduce into your business to achieve the same?

One thing that you might hear businesses saying is that 50% of their marketing works, they'd just love to know which 50%! Joking aside, there really is no excuse for not knowing your statistics these days, there are always ways of tracking where your business is coming from. A few years ago, when a business used display adverts, they could track which were working by giving the customer instructions like "call Jenny now". And, when the customer rang up and asked for Jenny, they knew the lead had come from a specific advert.

Now it's much simpler and you can get tracking numbers which are local phone numbers that only exist virtually but which automatically forward a call to your number when someone rings. They're such low cost that you can get a different number for each advert and at the end of the month, when you get the itemised bill, you can see just how many calls you've had off each.

I heard a story about a car sales business that was really struggling and when the owner was asked about what advertising he was doing and what this was bringing in, he had no idea. He decided to implement tracking numbers on his local paper adverts and let them run for a couple of months to see what was working. Across the term he was shocked to see that he didn't receive a single call on those numbers so he cancelled the adverts and saved himself £20,000 a year. That's a huge amount to put on your bottom line when you're struggling and if you can reinvest it in marketing that is working, just imagine the potential benefits.

The same goes for any other marketing you do, always have some way of tracking its success or failure, and whether offline or online always have a call to action on there, and make it time sensitive so people have to act now. If someone puts your literature or advert down without acting, the chance of them contacting you or purchasing your products drops significantly.

Literally everyone now has a website, however a lot of those websites are just a wasted opportunity and here's why. A website only really has two jobs, it's to sell stuff there-and-then to any visitors, and it's to capture details of the people visiting the website so that you can follow up and market to them more personally. If you have a website that does nether of those things then you're making a huge mistake.

Through your website you can get your existing and potential customers to understand the value you bring and what that ultimately means to them. I did some work with a really good quality builder, for example, who used only skilled tradespeople, quality materials, plus he'd give you a fixed price for each job because he gave accurate estimates. Now, he'd inevitably get undercut by other builders who didn't price the job properly, who used low quality products, cheap labour, or who knew that the work was going to run over and just charged as it happened – all of which meant that in many cases the client who'd chosen the cheaper builder paid very considerably more.

So how could my builder educate his potential clients and help them more honestly compare like for like? Well I asked him to produce a document which could be downloaded from his website in exchange for a name and email address. It was also something that he could send out to his prospective clients (in this case anyone in the area that had applied for planning permission), and alongside quotes.

The document focused on the seven questions to ask any builder and the three most common mistakes people make when engaging someone. This way he was able to gently educate his potential customers about the pitfalls that he knew were out there, and he came across not as someone who was complaining about the competition, or even as someone who wants to sell to the customer, but simply as someone helping them make an informed choice, that was best for them. Along with a few other tactics it worked a treat.

Now, if you're selling stuff online, make the process as simple as possible. Take Amazon as an example – that's a website that's got online selling absolutely nailed – just mirror their format and use their layout as a rough template for yourself and you can't go too far wrong. Have you seen the one-click function they have? Literally, you don't have to enter anything, you just log on (and it can remember all of your details), click purchase, and you're done. I've used it quite a few times when I've been in a conference or lecture and the speaker has referenced a book. Normally, before they've even finished talking about the book I've already ordered it, and it can sometimes dispatch before I leave the session. How brilliantly easy do they make it to buy from them.

Also, always, and I mean always, have a premier product. A premier product will normally be a much bigger uplift in profits for you and if you price it right, roughly 20% of your customers will buy it. Universal Studios in Orlando do this fabulously with an upgrade for their rides which was introduced a number of years ago. You pay an additional sum and you get to jump the main queues and short cut your way through to the start. They've priced it really carefully so that not too many people take it, ensuring the queues are always much shorter, and the only cost to them is a slightly different ticket and some rope dividers. Can you guess what the uplift is in profit is reported to be? $20 million dollars a year! And guess what, for the first 20 years they didn't have this really simple system in place (Ouch).

The best time to offer a premier product is when people have already committed to buy, and you'll see it a lot on websites. You've put in your payment details then you're asked you if you want the "professional" version of what you've just ordered, or an additional and complementary product, or even ongoing support. Something else you'll see – and again Amazon is brilliant at this – are the "people who bought this product also bought" suggestions where they may not be offering a premium product but may instead be trying to cross-sell you on another product using the information they've gathered on other people's spending habits to help them.

There's another TED talk that's well worth watching (actually there are hundreds so do explore every time you have a spare 10 to 20 minutes). Seth Godin's *How to Get Your Ideas to Spread* spells out why, when it comes to getting our attention, bad or bizarre ideas are more successful than boring ones. It's a great talk, full of examples of how being extreme grabs people's attention, how just being good isn't good enough, and how it can pay to go out on a bit of a limb.

And a great example of someone going out on a limb marketing-wise and not taking something as insignificant as having no money get in the way of his plans is Kenneth Cole. The now-famous shoe and fashion designer understood this point more than most, so when he was ready to launch his company back in the early 1980s he thought outside of the box big-time. Back then, the only way to target major shoe buyers during Market Week at the New York Hilton was to take a room at the hotel with more than 1,000 other companies, or hire a fancy showroom nearby – both requiring a budget that was completely out of the question.

Kenneth decided to borrow a 40foot long truck to solve his issue, but when he asked how he could get permission to park it on the prime spot of Sixth Avenue and 56th Street in New York City, he was told he categorically couldn't and that only utility companies or production companies shooting a film had any chance of a permit. Kenneth's response? He changed the name of his company to Kenneth Cole Productions – which it's still officially trading as today – and immediately filed a permit to shoot a film called 'The Birth of a Shoe Company'. He got his permit, got his mobile billboard and showroom, and – while he may not have produced any Oscar-winning movies over the past 30 years – within two and a half days of opening, he'd sold more than 40,000 pairs of shoes, had chronicled the birth of his company, and was well on the way to a phenomenally successful global business.

---

**Chapter Summary**

- Where do you sit in the marketplace?

- Have a premier product

- Develop and share advice and guidance about how to choose the ideal business with your clients

- Your website should either sell products or capture details.

---

# CHAPTER 9

## How to Sell More Stuff

It's funny how people love buying stuff but hate being sold to. Sales is certainly a real art form and, when it's done well, it makes the decision for the customer to say "yes" an easy one. When it's done badly though it's a car crash to see. Some people probably couldn't sell water to someone dying of thirst, and research shows us that 80% of lost sales are lost because nobody asked for it.

I did some work a while back with a client that I knew had been to see a potential client of theirs, so I asked them how things had gone . They replied "it went really well so I told him to think about it and left it with him". I didn't understand what there was to think about so we had a good discussion about asking for the sale and a few simple closes, (this was only our second meeting so we'd not covered it at that point). It's important that you're not too pushy but that you do encourage an answer – and many of us will be just like my client, who admitted that she was scared to ask in case she'd gotten a no.

We all have some fear of rejection, but if you really believe that the product or service the customer is looking at will benefit them, you're actually doing them a disservice by not asking. And if you tell someone to think about it, they will, and they'll probably also think about reasons not to go ahead with the purchase.

You might have seen this equation: D x V + FS = Sale. The D is the dissatisfaction or pain the customer has, V is the vision of what they want and FS is the first steps to get them to buy.

The idea is that you talk to the customer about their dissatisfaction, make that D as big as possible, really dig around to find out what it is that's paining them, get as much detail as possible, and ask them how it feels to be in that situation. Then start building the V vision and again make this huge, ask what that looks like, how it will feel, what that would do for them, what impact it would have on their life and family. Make the vision bold, and rich, and real, and the bigger you can make the D and V, the easier the sale will be. Now, this isn't about misleading people, it's simply about helping them to buy.

The FS, or first steps, is all about making the sale as much of a no brainer as you can. Think payment in instalments, offering a money-back guarantee, 30 day trial periods, free returns, in fact anything that you can do to get buy-in. Once your customers decide to buy a little, they're likely to go the whole way because once they've decided to buy from you, people like to feel like they've made the right decision and they'll look for evidence to support the decision.

There's a great book called *Yes! 50 Secrets from the Science of Persuasion* by Noah J. Goldstein, Steve J. Martin and Robert B. Cialdini, and it's got all sorts of interesting facts about persuasion and how getting small buy-ins from people could lead to much larger ones simply because people felt a connection and identified with the issue, campaign, or opportunity.

For one test they quoted, researchers knocked on 100 houses and asked if they could put a large placard in the front garden saying "kill your speed". Only 17% of householders said yes, and the others gave a flat no. Then, in a neighbouring, similar street, researchers knocked on the door and asked people if they could put a small sticker in their window saying "kill your speed". A huge 76% said yes and when, three days later, the researchers went back to the houses that had agreed to display the small stickers and asked if they'd now put a large placard in the front garden 53% of them said yes. That's more than triple the number of the neighbouring street.

The reasoning is that taking that small action, changed very slightly how these people viewed themselves. That little sticker in the window showed that they were the sort of person who cared about their community, and who didn't want people speeding, so when asked if they could put the much larger sign in the front garden many more identified with it and felt comfortable to say yes. Knowing that now, think about how can you get people to buy in to what you do, or spend just a little bit, because they'll then be much more likely to spend more with you later.

Think about your first step to engaging your customers like this. Do you let them have a free trial? Do you run a workshop? Do you offer a free health-check? Or is it simply a commercial introduction to you and your services? And do be honest. I'm not sure if you've ever done any cold calling but I heard a really great script someone was using which saw him win potential customers over with his honesty. It went something like this:

"Hi there I'm a local businessman. Look, I hate cold calling but it's the only way I can think of to get in touch with people like yourself, so if you can give me 30 seconds of your time I'd really appreciate it, and if at the end of that you don't think what I have will benefit you I'm happy to end the conversation."

If you use this script most people will give you 30 seconds, especially as they instantly connect with you because 99% of people also hate making cold calls, plus of course, you're local and a real person. This is a huge advantage for a lot of smaller businesses and it isn't used nearly often enough.

This also emphasises the importance of scripts and a sales process. If you have them and they're written down, it gives you something to measure your results against, and allows you to tweak them to see if you can improve your conversion ratio. Also, if you're anything like me you sometimes get lost in terms of what you're saying and a script will help keep you on track.

Say you're selling stationery and this is a price-based sale. As long as you're cheaper, the work should be yours, right? Or so you'd think. You go back to the customer and happily inform him that you're cheaper and he says, OK leave the quote with me and I'll get back to you. Now that's not great because you may end up with the situation where you're chasing him for an answer or worst case he sends your quote to a competitor and says "beat that". This whole situation can be avoided in most cases by simply explaining the process at the start and getting your potential client to agree to certain actions, should you be able to match what they're looking for.

In this scenario you could say something like "so what I'll do is go away and – with all the information I've taken – ensure that we can exactly match what you're looking for, and then I can come back next Tuesday. Now, as long as we're cheaper and can offer you the same or even a higher level of service than you're getting right now, are you happy to proceed so that we can actually look at getting things up and running?"

And just to make sure, when you ring to confirm the appointment you again repeat what you've already agreed. Perhaps say something like: "Hi David I'm just calling to confirm our appointment. We'll go through the paperwork and then as long as we're both happy we can look at getting up and running straight away". Now, if they come back with an objection like they're in a contract or their business partner needs to look over it before they sign, you can start to deal with the objections immediately rather than going to the meeting which may have worked out to be a waste of time.

Also, try and have different price points to appeal to different people. I was listening to a sales call recently and the guy was really good. He asked all the right questions to find out the potential client's dissatisfaction, built up the vision strongly and powerfully, and even got the guy agreeing that he needed to take action.

He was trying to sell him on a $17,000 all-done-for-you marketing package, but the potential customer was really honest and said there was no way for him to come up with that kind of cash. After a few more questions the sales guy sold him on a home study course that was $980. Now I don't actually think he sells many of those $17,000 packages, and I don't honestly believe that he expected to sell one to that client, but I bet he does sell loads of the $980 ones. It's such a huge price drop that someone will probably think "it's only $980" and it still goes some way to solving their dissatisfaction and moving them towards their vision.

I actually had someone do something similar in an airport recently. We were flying out to Egypt for a break as it was my partner's birthday just a few days later, and I saw that there was an Audi R8 up for raffle. She'd already decided that the R8 was going to be her next car, so I went up to buy a £13 raffle ticket to put in her card and make her smile. When I said that I wanted a ticket the guy on the stand said that he just needed to put my details on the system, and asked a few questions.

We chatted a bit while he inputted everything, then he said "how many do you want? 100?" Now I don't believe for a second that he's ever sold 100, so he came down to 10, then said he'd do me a deal for five tickets for £42 and I agreed. Remember I only went over for one ticket, he assumed I was buying multiples and acted that way. He was really good but he had a sales process and I expect that he did pretty well on the commission side of things.

I mentioned price earlier, and deep-down the majority of people don't want cheap, they want good value. A few years back I came across a story about one of the larger chains that sold kitchen utensils. They had a section with all the usual stuff, including two sets of pans – one was reasonably cheap and the other was more expensive – and as you'd imagine the majority of the sales were of the cheapish set. Then they introduced another set of pans which were really top of the range and very expensive, so customers now had a choice of three sets of pans when they came to purchase that item.

The interesting thing was that the majority of people now started buying the middle priced set of pans (the ones that used to be the most expensive) and they ignored the cheap set that was once the bestseller. Why was this? Well from a basic psychological level, the perception was that the cheap set couldn't be that great, they either couldn't afford or couldn't justify the expensive set, so they chose to go for the middle ones instead as they provided good value for money.

Just a warning on choices though, Barry Schwatz gave a talk on "The Paralysis of Choice: Why More is Less" where he showed that offering too many choices became a real negative. The customer ends up not being able to make a decision and they do nothing. Schwatz cites surveys done in supermarkets that showed, when customers were presented with a huge selection of brands of a certain item, fewer customers bought any items than when just a few were displayed. Ultimately, the wider selection led to a paralysis of choice where the customers just couldn't pick what to buy and as a result, they went away without choosing anything.

Something to be aware of is that it typically takes eight 'touches' from you before someone will buy from you. A 'touch' may be that you meet them networking, you send them an email, then you do a follow up call to see if you can send them something that might be of benefit, you send them the guide, perhaps they read some context-rich PR about you in a core magazine, they hear an interview with you on the local radio station, they visit your website, and then they receive a call from you to see if the guide was useful.

You can shortcut the process though if someone they know, like, and trust recommends you, but you need to have your sales process there to keep you on track and to allow you to tweak what you're doing as you evolve your process. If you aren't getting enough conversions off the back of your leads, try tweaking what you're doing to see if you can improve it.

Things like a *Seven Questions to Ask* and *The Three Most Common Mistakes People Make When Engaging* (insert whatever you are) guides will help, as will testimonials from previous clients – try and capture them on video if you can or at least include a photo of the person giving it next to the quote. If you do issue formal quotes to potential customers, send these testimonials with them, after all, people buy into what others say about you, more than what you say about you.

---

**Chapter Summary**

- The importance of a sales script and process

- You *can* have too many choices

- Clients need eight touches normally before they buy.

---

# CHAPTER 10

## Keep Your Customer Coming Back

It's not your customer's job to remember to purchase from you, it's your job to remind them. This can be one of the biggest failings of any business, with studies suggesting that around 68% of your customers will leave you because of perceived indifference. And if your customers think you don't care, they'll take their business to a competitor. Now, when you think how hard we work to provide people with our products and services, that's a bit shocking, especially if you look at the cost of keeping a customer compared with the cost of acquiring a new one.

However, this also provides one of the biggest opportunities we have, and I'm always on the look-out for businesses that really go the extra mile to interact with their customers as it gives me more great ideas that I can share with other businesses. Sadly though, more often than not it's the stuff that businesses aren't doing that seems to stand out.

Take my birthday. Me and my partner had a bit of a celebration, an overnight stay in a great hotel, a couple of meals out, some lovely pressies, all as you may expect. Now, despite the fact that we love eating out, socialising, and staying in nice hotels – and had been to numerous places over the previous twelve months – not a single one contacted us to offer birthday wishes and maybe an incentive for us to go and celebrate with them.

And I don't believe for a second that my birthday – which was mid-week, in the dead period after New Year and before the first pay check in January hits people's accounts – there weren't places that we'd eaten at previously that weren't quiet and that wouldn't have welcomed the extra custom. So what happened?

Two things could be going on here. Some of them simply didn't have our details. We'd been there, had a great meal and then they let us leave without even taking our names, which is a real shame. If they'd actually taken the time to come up with a system to capture our contact details it would've put them in a position to stay in touch and let us know what they're up to, plus they could share any special offers they might have.

Getting details isn't hard, you could offer to enter someone into a prize draw to win a meal or an overnight stay, tempt them with a free drink, or offer a reduction on their next purchase. Anything really, but just don't let them walk out without you having a way to get back in touch.

The second option is that they had indeed captured our contact details – and when I'm asked for these I pretty much always give them to businesses that I like – but then they completely failed to either stay in touch regularly, only did sporadic stuff that didn't have any kind of strategy behind it, or simply failed to capture important dates like birthdays and anniversaries.

If you're a restaurant owner and people eat with you three or four times a year, and you can instead get them to eat with you four or five times a year, that's roughly a 25%

increase in turnover and a lot more on your bottom line. All for a miniscule marketing cost. So, why aren't all businesses doing this? Yes, putting a database together can be time-consuming, and yes, doing regular newsletters and staying in touch will take some time out of your week or month, but if you look at the cost of acquiring a new customer compared to simply staying in touch with your existing customers, it's a no-brainer surely?

You should also segment your customers so that they receive information relevant to them. The more detailed your database, the easier it will be for you to do this. I recently had a national chain of stores put me on their email list after they got my details when I returned some products. Unfortunately, they kept sending me information on handbags and women's shoes. I stuck around for a few months as I thought they might start sending something through about men's products, but they didn't, so I unsubscribed.

And when you have a customer engaged, how can you reward loyalty? A great example of a company staying in touch with their customers is Charles Tyrwhitt, who well understand that men are a fickle lot and don't purchase shirts that often. They do a couple of things to make themselves stand out. The shirt catalogues not only have the products clearly displayed, they also succinctly explain the detail of the threading used on different shirts, the material used, the cuts… They're educating their customers about the shirts, not just trying to sell them.

They also make purchasing really easy – I can't always remember exactly what arm length or collar size I am because I tend to buy a few shirts all at the same time then not bother for ages, but it's not a problem for them as they have all of my measurements stored safely on their database, which removes the final obstacle for me to buy.

They also regularly send me catalogues through with special offers, and I recently received a letter from them thanking me for my purchase, awarding me a VIP card and saying how they were a family-run business (they are, but a very large one) and how much they appreciated my custom. It was a nice touch and I'll certainly be buying from them again.

Staying in touch is not about selling to people though. Yes of course you tell people about special offers and what's happening, but it's more about giving advice and guidance so that when a customer or prospective customer does think about your particular market or sector, they think about you. Tell people how to do what you do so that they can do it for themselves, and what you'll find is that those with money would rather you do it because they value their time and they want to make sure that it's done properly.

Even those who choose to do it themselves this time, for whatever reason, will still think of you the next time that job comes around, and they may be in a position then to engage you. So do send regular newsletters, plus, if you see something and you think your clients would benefit from it, do send it out to them.

I know a bakery that every now and then has a bit of a slow day. Now typically in this kind of industry, stuff will pass its sell-by-date quickly and have to be thrown away, but not so with these guys. They made sure to capture the mobile numbers of virtually all of their customers, and if it looks like they're carrying too much stock at a certain point in the afternoon – and they think that there could be waste – they send a text out to all of their customers offering them a third off whatever it is they have too much of. Not only does this prevent much – or often any – waste, but customers often purchase other items while they're there and so other sales improved too.

If you're staying in touch with people make sure that you make full use of what's happening on the calendar – whether that's Mother's Day, St. Patrick's Day, Easter, Back to School, Christmas, or any of the number of the other celebrations scheduled across the year. Is there some way that you can get involved and get people spending with you? I work with an artisan sausage roll producer and supplier that does a special almost every month. When they take a client's order they always mention that they're doing, say, a Guinness and Ale sausage roll to celebrate St Patrick's Day, and pretty much every time the client adds an extra few requests for the special too.

Talking about special offers, the book *Yes!* I mentioned earlier shared a really interesting story of a car wash which gave out loyalty cards to customers. After eight car washes within a certain time-frame, the ninth was free, but what they did was design and distribute two different cards as a trial – the first had eight squares on the back which needed to be stamped, and the second had ten but they stamped the first two so that the customer felt like they had a bit of a head start.

What they found was that even though both cards needed eight stamps to get the free car wash, of the customers who had the ten-boxed card with two stamps already marked in, a higher percentage came back, they visited more often, and more actually qualified for the free wash than those that were just given the card with eight boxes.

Why? Well the customers felt that they were getting something of more value with the card that needed ten stamps, plus by giving them two stamps to start them off, the car wash evoked the law of reciprocity, which sees us all feel a real desire to repay any favours we're offered. Think of the power of working this into your business.

And this links to an interesting discovery an alternative therapy client of mine made recently. When making appointments their receptionist would write out the appointment card and give it to the person, but typically they had around 20% of patients with appointments cancel or not show up. They trialled a change which saw the receptionist hand the card and a pen to the patient themselves, and she encouraged them to write the appointment details down. Simple indeed, but would you believe that the no-show rate dropped to just 10%, such is the power of actively engaging with your customers. You see, when we write something out we link to the unconscious mind and make a higher level of commitment.

Just think about how you can you build this into your business – how can you encourage your current and prospective customers to sign something or write something out themselves to engage this higher level of commitment? And this is another reason why I always insist on plans and goals been written out, because the chances of achieving what you write down increase dramatically when compared with just having something in your head.

It's really important that you stay in touch with your customers, and social media can be a great way of doing just that and of seeing what your clients are up to. But, if you're going to commit to social media as a tool then please make sure that you have a strategy and that you are consistent – there's little worse than someone having a social media account and then not responding to messages or updating it. People will notice and it will do more harm than not having one at all.

I saw a business coach that was running a series of master-classes recently, one of which was on social media, but if you looked at his website the last tweet was two months old. It doesn't give a great impression does it. Set up feeds across your social media platforms to search for your business name and your own name to see what's being said about you, and remember that time moves quicker online and people expect a response within a far shorter timeframe than in the real world.

Virgin is great at this. I heard a story about a guy who was stuck on a stationary train and posted a sarcastic comment on Twitter. Within just a few minutes, a Virgin customer service representative had tweeted back to ask where he was travelling to, before responding to explain why the train had been held up and apologising. It didn't change what was happening but the guy felt better for someone actually caring enough to respond to him, and he's since told hundreds of people how impressed he was – and now I'm telling you all. Good move Virgin!

**Chapter Summary**

- Capture everyone's details

- Segment your customers and stay in touch

- Reward loyalty.

# CHAPTER 11

## Step One, Start With
## The End In Mind

Now this isn't the largest section of the book but it is the most important bit of the book. This is what the majority of businesses lack and it's exactly what we're going to put right.

Remember how earlier we talked about things being *important-and-urgent* and that what's *important* should never get sacrificed for what's *urgent*? Well, building your overall strategy and plan is super-important, I'd suggest that you read through the next few pages once or twice, and then that you set aside at few hours in your diary to work through the whole process. Treat this as an appointment with your most important client...You!

The next five steps are about developing a strategy and plan to really give you focus. I'd also suggest and that you involve others who have a vested interest in your business success. That could be business partners, your senior management, spouses or life partners, whoever is important to you. Ask them to challenge you and offer potential solutions.

|       | NOW | TWO YEARS | FIVE YEARS |
|-------|-----|-----------|------------|
| **B**<br>**U**<br>**S**<br>**I**<br>**N**<br>**E**<br>**S**<br>**S** |     |           |            |
| **L**<br>**I**<br>**F**<br>**E**<br>**S**<br>**T**<br>**Y**<br>**L**<br>**E** |     |           |            |

Draw this out on a flip chart pad or on a large piece of paper. We've already covered why it's important to really get an understanding of what lifestyle you want, so this is where you really nail it down.

In five years time what do you want your life to look like? Think about where you're living. What type of house do you have? How many bedrooms are there? How is it all furnished? What does your garden look like? Do you have outbuildings? And pets? What about an orchard, a lake or a swimming pool?... You get the picture. Make this a really rich image and note *everything* down.

Now think about your working week. What does that look like? How many holidays are you taking? How are you getting there (and remember that this is in five years so you can set whatever target you want)? How many long weekends are you taking and which destinations are you travelling to? What cars are you driving? What colour are they? What do the interiors look like? Do you have any other vehicles like a motorbike, jet ski, or track day car?

And what else is going on? Have you written a book? Do you have a property portfolio? Have you had children? Or maybe you're sending ones you already have to private school? Perhaps you've learnt to fly, or you're doing more of a hobby that you love? Really get a feel for what you want and put down absolutely everything that you can think of.

Now, what does your business need to do to provide you with that standard of living (and remember that this stuff doesn't have to be paid for outright – although it can of course). What profits do you need to generate? What turnover is required? And what staffing levels? What premises do you need and do you own them? Do you need vehicles and loading bays? Think about everything that your business will require at that point.

And now write out where you are today in terms of both your lifestyle and your business, and where you'll need to be in roughly three years for all the areas we've already got on the sheet.

# Step Two, Build Your Overall Business Strategy

Your strategy is there to give you a feel for what's happening within your business over these next five years. Work out each year on a flip chart pad or large piece of paper, and build up the picture of everything that's going on in your business. Start at the five year point and work backwards, you can even use post-it notes if you want, that way you can take them off if it doesn't look right as you build your picture.

Start with your profit and turnover then look at all the different areas of your business such as marketing, sales, premises, staff, distribution, target clients, geographical areas, operational challenges, product areas, product percentages... To make it as easy as possible for you, I've produced a list of things below and shared some specifics that you may want to include in your strategy diagram:

## Marketing

Think back to the marketing plan section where we asked you to build up an avatar for your ideal clients. So, where are you marketing? Where are your competitors advertising? Is there somewhere else your clients are that they've missed? Are there any awards you need to be going for? What kind of PR are you doing to raise your profile? How is your marketing building over the next few years? How many different marketing strategies are you going to need (and remember, you must track them all). Are you going international?...

## Product or Services

What products or services are you going to be offering? How many different types? How are these going to change as time moves on? What bolt-ons, upgrades, or added-value items are you going to add to them?...

## Distribution

What percentage of the products or services you're offering account for your business? It may be that you're looking to increase the percentage of a certain product because it's more profitable for example…

## Geographic Areas

Which areas are you looking to focus on? Are you staying in your own county, district or state? If so, which towns are you targeting first? Or are you going wider? Which regions of the country are core to you? And how is that going to develop over the next few years? Are you going international?...

## Operations

What kind of staff, services or production systems are you going to develop? What size and scope? And what are the potential issues?

## Premises

Are you in rented premises or have you bought your own? What size of premises do you need for your staffing or production requirements and when will this need to change from present-day? Would a purpose-built facility be an advantage? And do you need to move to a certain area to help with recruitment, for distribution reasons, or to benefit from better road and rail links?

**Sales**

Is the first step to develop a sales process and scripts? Do you need to set up how you're going to track and measure success? Will you attend sales trainings, and if so which ones and focused on what? How many sales staff are you going to employ?...

**Customers**

Who are your customers? Where are they located? How many of them are there? Do you have ten small ones then two really large ones, or twenty massive ones straight away? (Make sure that at no time is your business at the mercy of just one major customer – if you bring on a customer that's 30% of your business, well done, but feel panicked enough to go and get another one of an equal or even larger size so that if they left you, you wouldn't be in trouble).

**Funding Issues**

Where is the funding for growth coming from? How much do you need? Is the business producing enough or are you going to need outside investment? What do you need to do now to be able to secure that funding in the future?

Start from where you'll be in five years time and work your way to present day. And try to think how each different area will affect each other area of the business. One client I worked with realised that he'd actually need to move premises within 18 months because his production was going to outstrip the area he had available to work in. And with timings as they were, he actually only had six months from our strategy day to find somewhere.

Without thinking ahead and planning like this, it may have been a year before he realised and then he'd certainly have experienced some pain – whether struggling to get premises and move in time, or having to slow down production or turn work away because his existing site couldn't cope.

So, looking at where you are now, look at what you need to be doing next year. Do you need to hire administrative staff? Move premises to become more efficient? Give your staff more training or a pay rise? Will there be additional costs such as utilities? Will you be moving to an even higher standard of work, or will you secure accreditation so that you can charge more? Perhaps you'll aim to get the cost of sales down by a few percent? Or, if you're purchasing more, you may wish to negotiate a better deal or a discount from your suppliers….

If you can't make the figures work on paper its unlikely that you'll make them work in real life, so go back to the drawing board and start again until it does all add up. And also do just be aware of what we term "bonkernomics" when you're setting your figures. Many of us will have seen a Dragons Den episode where an entrepreneur is pitching their idea to the Dragons and values their business in the £multiple-millions despite them doing limited research, not yet launching – or often even making – a product, and without boasting any assets at all. Dream big when it comes to lifestyle, but apply a reality check when it comes to your business statistics.

Now you've got a rough map of what you're doing for the next three to five years, leave that in sight for the moment so you can refer back to it. I'd suggest sticking it on a wall somewhere prominent.

# Step Three, Plan and Analysis

T his is where we look at the overall strategy you've just built up and start to lay out what needs to be done in the business to achieve these targets.

So, look at each of the areas you've just worked through, such as marketing, staffing, and premises, and using your flip chart paper start making a list of things that need to be done on the left hand side of the page (so, for example you might need to get some sort of accreditation within your industry to charge more for your services, do this for every area).

Once you have all the things that you need to do, start to think about what challenges there are around those things you need to achieve and list those on the right hand side of the flip chart. You might, for example, need to spend £10,000 training someone up to achieve your accreditation and you may also then be at risk of them leaving the business. Again, do this for every area weve covered in your business.

Once this is done you have a pretty good feel for what needs to be achieved and what some of the potential challenges could be on this jorney so we shouldn't get too many nasty suprises. Particularly as the next step should take care of pretty much everything on this list...

# Step Four, Build Your Action List

Now that you've completed the analysis we can start to build a plan of how we're actually going to drive your business forward on a day-to-day basis. So, you can now move away from the flip chart and use an old fashioned pen and paper and, looking at your plan and analysis, what action can you take about each of the things you've written down? So, if you have a real need to get that accreditation, write it on your action list and consider whether there any other accreditations you should be thinking about too…

Now, consider the challenges that you've noted down as potentially facing and consider these in more detail. In our example of gaining acccrediation, the cost might be a challenge but then you have to look at the return on investment over the long term. We also mentioned that the person you train might decide to leave, so what can you do to get them to commit to your business, and what can you offer them?

The idea is to either take action about something or accept it as it is. For example, if you've put down a meteor hitting the earth as a challenge to your business, there's probably not much you can do about that so you may have to accept that for what it is. However, if one of the challenges was that you're in a partnership and you still haven't got a shareholders' agreement and cross party options done, then that absolutely must be listed for action.

Build up a list of things that you need to do to ultimately get you to the lifestyle you want, and don't hold back. Think of how you can achieve these things, and not the reasons why it wouldn't happen to you. Also, go back over the strategy you built for the business and see if there is anything on there that you need to transfer as an action, just in case you've missed something.

And when you've done all of that... take a break! Your head might be slightly frazzled but the last few hours will have been amongst the most valuable that you've spent on your business to-date.

# Step Five, Pulling It All Together

OK, so you now need to transfer the overall Business Strategy and your Plan from the flip chart onto paper so you can refer back to them. For the Business Strategy I'd suggest writing it out as a timeline so you can see how the business builds up and how all the different pieces fit together. I'd also suggest printing two copies of each of these, one for a folder and one for the wall.

Now, we also really need to start building your list of actions for the next year and this is where the Project Log download from the website can be used. Look at what you've produced, and what needs to be achieved by the end of the year for you to hit your targets.

Again using our securing accreditation example, you might have a few tasks to complete that require action, like selecting the right person for training, offering incetives to tie them into the business, raising funding… These tasks will need to be completed in a certain order and you can set this out on a month-by-month basis.

I've included a Project Plan and the Break Through Line of Sight Plan, that you can download for free on the website to accompany this book, so do download it and you can use either of these, it's down to personal choice, you'll see that I've already provided an example. You can then start to build up a picture of how these actions across the whole business start to tie in together. Once you've set out the actions and tasks, you can also print off these pages and put them in your folder or even on the wall.

In your folder you should now have a Business Plan that you can look at. It won't be one of those huge business plans or tick-box exercises that sit on a shelf and gather dust. Rather, it'll be a practical and dynamic one page Business Strategy. Your Plan shares your targets for the next five years, and your one or two-page Project Log shows your actions for the next phase of your growth.

**Chapter Summary**

- Where do you want to be in five years?

- Develop your Business Strategy

- Complete your Plan and Analysis

- Create your action list

- Finalise your Project Log and transfer your Business Strategy and Plan to paper

# CHAPTER 12

## Wrapping Up

So, you've worked out your strategy, you've developed your plan, and you can now focus on the actions that will get you the lifestyle and business you deserve. But there's one huge risk with what you've just done and that is a failure to implement. I'd suggest putting time aside every single work day from here-on, say the first 60 or preferably 90 minutes to work *on* your business not *in* it. Don't even open your emails as that will distract you, just sit down and start working on the activity from your plan. That one habit, compounded over the next few years, will help you take massive strides towards what you're looking to achieve.

If you're anything like me you'll have always achieved results when you've been held accountable or when you've been working through a programme, so get someone to hold you accountable. Invest in yourself. Read business, skills and self-development books and listen to audio programmes. After all, Jim Rohn was absolutely right when he said: "the difference between where you are today and where you'll be in five years from now will be found in the quality of books you've read."

You might not always be able to fully control who you mix with, but you can absolutely control what you read or listen to. If you had an opportunity to talk with Richard Branson about business I'm sure that you'd jump at the chance. So why not read his books or listen to some of his interviews and imagine that he's actually there with you (remember, the brain doesn't know the difference).

No matter who you look at in the world, anyone at the top of their game almost always has a variety of coaches and experts to help them stay on track. Think about any sportsperson, athlete, or racer, and business is no different. Less than 4% of businesses make it to the financial security they want, another 16% are doing really well, while 60% are getting by, and 20% are left really struggling. Think about which statistic you want to be…

Now, if you're sitting there thinking "well I'm not particularly interested in being one of the top earners", or if you don't believe you can be, the bad news is that you still have to be really good to earn a comfortable living and work reasonable hours, so start investing in yourself now. Your brain and its thinking, if introduced to an idea (even if it doesn't believe that idea) will see your thinking stretched and eventually, over time, you'll start having bigger ideas, doing things on auto pilot, believing that you can be all you've ever wanted.

I sincerely wish every success to you, your family, and your business. I'd love to stay in touch if you want to, and to hear about your own successes using the tools in this book. As I develop new programmes and support that will be of use to you I'll let you know, and if you want to be added to the prestigious ranks of the *Survive to Thrive Success Board*, do send me a picture and a few lines about where you were and where you are now. You can also follow me on Pinterest (AlanHorizons) for business tips and insights, inspirational words, and my own favourite resources like must-watch TED talks.

Have a great year and here's wishing you every success with your plan, your focus, and getting the life you deserve.

---

## "Claim Your <u>FREE</u> Business Builder Tools For Use In Your Business and Increase Your Turnover by 50% to 100% Without Spending More Money On Advertising!"

*(£297 Total Value)*

### *Details revealed below...*

**Alan S Adams,** author and leading business consultant, is offering an incredible opportunity for you to improve the way you run your business, without spending more money on advertising for <u>FREE</u>! Alan has used these systems to help businesses grow for years, and he is so confident that they work, he always offers a **"500% Return On Investment or Your Money Back Guarantee"**. So claim your free tools today and discover:

- How to **quickly increase your sales by 50% to 100%** without spending more money on advertising

- How to **guarantee that your business grows** with small changes achieving huge returns

- The **"Five Simple Steps"** to get you a plan, really get you focused, and get you building the lifestyle you deserve

- **Secret insider tips and techniques** to get more new customers, and get your past customers to come back into your business and buy from you again and again

- How to get **Free Business Building** tools that have helped countless other businesses grow, and that Alan uses with his private clients.

*Claim Your FREE Tools by Visiting:*

**www.alansadams.com/free**

# About The Author

A former weapons engineer and submariner with the Royal Navy, Alan S Adams now channels his expertise to get beneath the surface of business strategy in his role as Founder and Director of Horizons Consultants.

A Master Neuro-Linguistic Programming (NLP) practitioner and fully qualified life coach, Alan has a real passion for understanding business which was heightened by studying for a BSc Degree in International Disaster Engineering and Management at Coventry University, where he focused on companies' and governments' strategies to deal with crises.

He now uses these skills to provide strategic support, to coach and train business owners across the length and breadth of the UK, in particular small and medium-sized enterprises. Alan runs a series of seminars, workshops, and interactive sessions where business owners can receive practical advice and guidance in areas such as increasing business profitability and cashflow, goal-setting, and business growth. He also works with companies on a more strategic level, where he conducts a complete top to bottom review, and then works with business owners to analyse their strengths and weaknesses, before putting in place and delivering bespoke business development plans.

Shropshire born and bred, and now living in Telford, Alan is something of an adrenaline junkie. He is a keen snowboarder and motorcyclist, and also enjoys taking part in outdoor activities such as skydiving.

# Here's What People Say About Alan S Adams

**Jo Carroll**
**Founder and Creative Director of Giant Creative**
"Alan really is the man to speak to for the times when you need to stop, take stock and review what direction you and your business is moving in. He helps bring clarity and focus by setting out a clear plan for the path ahead"

**Andy Rao**
**Managing Director of Key 3 Media**
"Alan's Masterclass workshops have been instrumental in the growth of my business, enabling me to focus more on the company rather than being in it"

**Darren Taylor**
**Managing Director of Rainbow Safety Signs**
"Alan has made a massive difference to my company and I would recommend Alan to anybody who wants to move their business forward"

**Charlie Hutton**
**Founder and Director of Hutchinson Web Design**
"I always had loads of ideas, and considered myself pretty focused, but working with Alan really took everything to another level and has driven my business forward at a pace that's blown me away, I can highly recommend him"

**Julian Smout**
**Managing Director Verve**
"I worked with Alan twelve months ago, since then my business has tripled insize, if you're looking to grow your business, I can highly recommend him"

**Rhiannon Williams**
**Client Services Director of Zen Communications**
"Alan has had such a positive influence on both my business life and personal life, and I would encourage anybody who feels they need a steer in the right direction to get in touch with him"

**Anthony Digweed**
**Owner and Founder of Monkhide**
"What I've learnt from Alan will directly benefit my business, by helping us to focus on planning for future growth"

**Catherine Buckley**
**Best Of Shrewsbury**
"Alan is fun! You don't feel like you are being preached too but rather shown the right path, it's clear that he really knows his stuff and techniques, so enjoy the process"

**Leanne Crowther**
**Director of Little Round Cake Company**
"It's frustrating as we know what we should be doing as a business, but what Alan gives you is a kick up the bum and re-energises you to focus on what's important"

**Gaynor Hand**
**Director of Orange Consultancy**
"Alan's reminded me again to focus on the goal, rather than the slog to get to it, just what I needed at this moment, thank you"